BIBLE
THEN & NOW

BIBLE
THEN & NOW

JENNY ROBERTS

MACMILLAN • USA

A QUARTO BOOK

MACMILLAN
A Simon & Schuster Macmillan Company
1633 Broadway
New York, NY 10019-6785

Library of Congress Cataloging-in-Publication Data

Roberts, Jenny, 1944–
    Bible then & now / Jenny Roberts.
        p.   cm.
    "A Quarto book" – T.p. verso.
    Includes bibliographical references and index.
    ISBN 0-02-861347-3
    1. Bible–Antiquities.   2. Mediterranean Region–Antiquities.
    3. Church history–Primitive and early church, ca. 30–600.
    4. Jews–History–To A.D. 70.   I. Title.
BS621.R63   1996
220.9' 5–dc20   96–12243
                                                                    CIP

The book was designed and produced by
Quarto Inc.
The Old Brewery
6 Blundell Street
London N7 9BH

SENIOR EDITORS Michelle Pickering, Maria Morgan
SENIOR ART EDITOR Elizabeth Healey
EDITOR Ralph Hancock
DESIGNER Liz Brown
ACETATES Leen Ritmeyer, Kevin Maddison, Gary Cross
ILLUSTRATORS Sally Bond, Janice Nicholson
CALLIGRAPHY Annie Moring
PHOTOGRAPHERS Paul Forrester, Laura Wickenden
PICTURE RESEARCHER Susannah Jayes
PICTURE RESEARCH MANAGER Giulia Hetherington
EDITORIAL DIRECTOR Mark Dartford
ART DIRECTOR Moira Clinch

Typeset by Central Southern Typesetters, Eastbourne, UK
Manufactured by Regent Publishing Services Ltd, Hong Kong
Printed by New Island Printing Co. Ltd, Hong Kong

"Biblical theology and Biblical archeology
must go hand in hand if we are to
comprehend the Bible's meaning"

G.E. Wright, *Biblical Archeologist*, 1957

CONTENTS

Introduction   8

Map   16

BABYLON – Nebuchadrezzar's city, 5th century BC   18

The Sea of Galilee   26

ATHENS – The Acropolis, 5th century BC   28

HEBRON – Tomb of the Patriarchs, 1st century BC   36

The Philistines   42

BETHLEHEM – Church of the Nativity, 6th century AD   44

Lost Treasures of the Old Testament   52

DAMASCUS – Straight Street, 1st century AD   54

Moses in Egypt   62

EPHESUS – The great theater, 2nd century BC   64

NINEVEH – Sennacherib's city, 7th century BC   70

The Persian Empire   78

CYPRUS – Roman gymnasium at Salamis, 1st century AD   80

Mountains of the Old Testament   88

JERICHO – Herod's palace, 1st century BC   90

The River Jordan   98

CAESAREA – Ancient harbor in New Testament times   100

TYRE – Hadrian's Arch, 1st century AD   106

Joseph in Egypt   114

JOPPA – Ancient port, 1st century BC   116

The Garden of Eden   122

CAPERNAUM – Synagogue, 4th century AD   124

The Samaritans   130

JERUSALEM – Herod's Temple, 1st century BC   132

The Passion of Jesus   140

Index   142

Credits   144

INTRODUCTION

A book about "Bible places then and now" poses two questions. Where are the Bible places? When was "then"? We tend to think of the Bible narratives as being set in one small area that we call "the Holy Land," and we have a vague notion of a period that we label "Bible times." In fact, there is enormous diversity in both time and place.

Where are the Bible places?

It is true that the history of the Jewish people as related in the Old Testament is set mainly in a very small area between the eastern Mediterranean and the desert. The promised land of Canaan, or Palestine, stretching "from Dan to Beersheba," is only about 150 miles (240 km) long. Genesis describes how the Patriarchs settled in that land, where God promised them that they would father a great nation. Exodus tells how Moses led the Jews back to the promised land; and the book of Joshua relates the fight to take the land, and how it was divided between the tribes. Eventually a kingdom was established with Jerusalem as its capital, but this was later divided into a northern kingdom of Israel and a southern kingdom of Judah. Much of the rest of the Old Testament is concerned with the continuous wars and strife

*In the Sinai region, little has changed since Biblical times. A barren tree stands in the desert (**above**), while a Bedouin tent illustrates the nomadic lifestyle of the present-day population (**right**).*

between the Jewish tribes of Israel and Judah and the surrounding peoples, and with the Jews' constant struggle to retain their land. To understand this history is to grasp the basis of present-day Middle Eastern politics.

Although the land of Israel itself was relatively small, the world of the Bible was very much larger. All the regions bordering present-day Israel – what we now call Jordan, Lebanon, Syria, and Egypt – feature significantly in the Old Testament. The first great nation to impinge on the lives of the Jews was Egypt. After Joseph was sold into slavery there, a Jewish population grew up in the land, and by the time Moses was born they were greatly oppressed by the powerful Egyptians. But the countries that eventually destroyed Israel and Judah were Assyria (now Syria) and Babylon (in what is now Iraq). The Babylonian Empire was later conquered by Persia (now Iran).

Although Jesus' ministry was centered on a small area, the New Testament expands the Bible world to include Europe, for it was the Roman Empire that now dominated the entire Mediterranean region. After Jesus' death the Apostles began missionary ventures that took them through much of that empire: to Turkey, Greece, Cyprus, Malta, and Rome itself.

All synagogues contain ornamental Torahs like these; they contain the Pentateuch – the first five books of the Bible – handwritten on parchment scrolls. The Torah scrolls are taken from the sanctuary and read from every Sabbath and on Holy Days.

When were the Bible times?

It is impossible to date the earliest events of the Bible. The chronology provided by the Bible itself cannot be relied on independently of other writings and archeological evidence. The stories of Adam and Eve, Cain and Abel, Noah and the flood, belong to prehistory and share many elements of universal myths. It is unlikely that Abraham could have lived any earlier than 2000 BC, and there is some evidence that the "Patriarchal" age started a century or more later than this. Joseph probably lived some time between 1750 and 1650 BC, and the Exodus from Egypt and the conquest of the promised land is thought to have taken place in the 13th century BC.

The period when the Judges ruled in Israel lasted until 1050 BC, when Saul became king, and the kingdom was divided about 120 years later. The northern kingdom, now called

Paul took the gospel message throughout the Roman Empire. St Paul's Pillars and the Basilica stand in the ancient city of Paphos in Cyprus.

Israel, and the city of Samaria fell in about 720 BC, and then in about 586 BC the southern kingdom, Judah, and Jerusalem fell and the Jews were taken into captivity in Babylon. The captivity, the Jews' return, and the re-building of Jerusalem are the subject of the last part of the Old Testament, which takes us up to about 430 BC.

The New Testament covers a period lasting about 100 years, from the reign of Herod the Great, during which time Jesus was born, to the end of the "Apostolic" age, with the deaths of the Apostles occurring mainly between AD 60 and 100.

How did they live?

When we consider that Bible times stretched over a period as long as that between the birth of Jesus and the present day, it is clear that there must have been many changes and developments in the culture and civilization over that time. However, we cannot compare the changes of those days with the rapid developments of more recent history. Many aspects of daily life, such as work, clothes, housing, and family structure, saw little change over those 2,000 years.

The Bible starts in the Middle Bronze Age, with the first settlers of Palestine living a seminomadic life, moving with their flocks from place to place in search of fresh pastures and water, setting up their tents for a while, and then moving on. Society was based on the extended family, ruled by a patriarch. Most marriages were monogamous but it was not uncommon for men to take second wives or concubines, particularly if this was the only way to produce an heir.

Several cities already existed at the start of the second millennium BC. In Canaan itself Jerusalem, Jericho, Shechem, and several other cities were settled, and here people lived in houses rather than tents. Houses, often built into the city wall, were solidly constructed of stone and timber, although in the villages they might be made of stone and mud or sometimes just mud. They were used not only as dwelling places, but to house animals, to keep agricultural stores, and as workplaces for various kinds of industry, such as grinding grain or weaving and dyeing cloth.

Egypt, at the time when Joseph was taken there, was a very much more advanced civilization than the one he came from. The third millennium BC had seen a rapid advance in prosperity and culture; this was when the great pyramids were constructed. Architecture, literature, and art had already developed to high levels, and there was a complex political structure with kings ruling through priests and civil servants.

From the period when the kingdoms were established, towns became of greater importance in Israel. These took their status from the fact that they were fortified, not from their size. Most were very small with around 1,000 people crowded into them; there were no paved streets, merely narrow alleys between the houses. Often there was an overspill of people living in tents outside the towns. Life was still mainly agricultural, with many people moving away from the towns in the summer to live on the land. Housing for most people remained very modest, but architecture developed with the great building program that Solomon embarked on to create the temple in Jerusalem, as well as palaces for himself and his household.

Below: This copper ingot showing a man carrying an ox hide comes from a Bronze Age incense-burner found on the island of Cyprus. **Bottom:** *Cosmetic jars, a comb, and kohl spoons were among the many archeological treasures excavated at Masada, site of a Herodian fortress and palace.*

Ordinary people traveled on foot, with donkeys used mainly as beasts of burden. Horse-drawn chariots were used only by armies and the very rich; the poor roads of the time made wheeled vehicles impractical for serious journeys.

The main occupation of the people of Palestine was agriculture, although much of the land was desert and uncultivable, and even the fertile areas were sometimes affected by drought and plagues of locusts. Sheep and goats were raised, and wheat, barley, olives, vines, and many kinds of fruits and vegetables were grown. Other occupations included the processing, dyeing, spinning, and weaving of woolen and linen cloth; mining, mainly of copper; and various kinds of craft work, including pottery, leatherwork, and metalwork. Fishing did not become a major occupation until New Testament times, when an important industry grew up around the Sea of Galilee.

The great conquerors of the Jewish people, the Assyrians and the Babylonians, were very much richer and more advanced, with life

A timeless scene: the River Jordan, north of Lake Galilee.

centered on the great cities, which were well laid out with paved streets and impressive public buildings. There was a greater diversity of trade and industry, and all kinds of goods – precious metals, linen, spices – were exported.

By New Testament times the main change that had occurred in Israel was the constant presence of the occupying Romans. Although the Jews resented their new masters as oppressors, the Romans brought new peace and stability to what had for so long been a troubled area. They built many fine paved roads and erected public buildings, such as administrative offices, markets, and baths, in the towns. All these had to be paid for by heavy taxes, which made the Romans – and the tax collectors – very unpopular.

The more developed areas of the Roman Empire, the cities of Greece and Asia Minor (now modern Turkey), became familiar to Paul and the other Apostles. The inhabitants of these cities led sophisticated lives, attending theaters, athletic events, and political

These leather sandals were found at Masada, near the Dead Sea. They probably belonged to one of the Jewish rebels opposing Roman rule, who occupied Herod's fortress between AD 66–73.

meetings and debates. Religion and philosophy were important to them but, unlike the old Jewish and the new Christian religions, the worship of the gods of Greece and Rome was mainly ritual and had no real influence on the way the people lived their lives.

How do we know?

Of course, most of what is known about Bible times and places has always come from internal evidence from the Bible itself. Some extra facts have emerged from the writing of ancient historians, such as the Jewish historian Josephus in the 1st century AD. But our knowledge has increased immensely in the last couple of centuries through the work of Biblical archeologists.

Travelers and pilgrims had been visiting the Holy Land for centuries, and there had been some serious attempts to locate those Bible places whose site was unknown. In the 19th century, when the study of antiquities became extremely popular, there were several archeological expeditions to Jericho and Jerusalem; but most scholars concentrated on the great lands surrounding Palestine, looking for discoveries from ancient Egypt, Assyria, and Babylon. One of the most exciting finds from this period was the library of Ashburnipal in Nineveh.

It was not until the end of the 19th century that archeology became a serious science. Sir William Flinders Petrie, excavating near Gaza, realized that the pieces of pottery he found at different heights above sea level differed significantly from each other. He evolved a system of dating finds according to the pottery found at the same level; this method proved to be remarkably accurate and was developed and used extensively by later archeologists. By the middle of the 20th

The message of the first Christian missionaries had to compete with the older Greek and Roman religions. This marble statue depicts Aphrodite, goddess of love.

A statue of the Roman emperor Hadrian, found at Tell Shalem in Israel. In AD 134 Hadrian suppressed the Jewish revolt against the Roman Empire, led by Bar Kokhba.

East make this a difficult and sometimes dangerous place to work. And of course, as with all archeology, it is not possible simply to piece together all the evidence from excavations and come up with an accurate picture of how people lived in ancient times. Most organic materials will have rotted; it is a matter of chance as to what will survive.

Some of the most exciting finds of the 20th century have been in Egypt and the cities of the Mesopotamian area. These places were highly developed civilizations when the people of Palestine were simple nomadic tribespeople. In the biblical Ur of the Chaldees, in modern Iraq, the city where Abraham once lived, Sir Leonard Woolley discovered thousands of clay tablets recording civic history, and ancient royal graves containing beautifully crafted weapons and decorative objects of gold and precious stones. The sites of the ancient cities of Nineveh and Babylon have yielded some extraordinary finds, which are discussed in this book. The discoveries in Egypt in the 1920s of Tutankhamun's tomb and many other treasures throw light on the Egypt of Moses' day.

Apart from the work on Jericho, the greatest archeological breakthroughs in Israel itself have been Masada and the Dead Sea Scrolls. In the 1960s Israeli archeologists excavated Masada, west of the Dead Sea, where Herod had built a fortress and palaces. The excavations revealed much of the structure of these Herodian buildings, and also yielded evidence of the occupation of the fortress by Jewish zealots defying the Romans from AD 66 to 73.

The Dead Sea Scrolls were discovered at Qumran, a wadi (watercourse) northwest of the Dead Sea. In 1947 a shepherd discovered

century a new technique had been developed: stratigraphy, which involved a minute examination of the soil within each level of earth. It was developed by Sir Mortimer Wheeler and Dame Kathleen Kenyon, and used by the latter in her work at Jericho and at Jerusalem.

Biblical archeology is fraught with problems. It has been easiest to study those places that have fallen into ruins, because of the obvious difficulty of excavating in an inhabited town. There are further problems in those places that have sacred connections for Jews, Christians, or Muslims, where disturbing a site might be considered sacrilegious. Also, the ever-present tensions in the Middle

some jars in a cave, containing cloth and parchment scrolls. An American scholar working in Jerusalem identified the writing on the scrolls as Hebrew texts. One was a copy of the book of Isaiah that turned out to be about 1,000 years older than any existing Hebrew text. Although 15 or so of the scrolls have been translated, many were in tiny fragments and it looked as though the task of fitting them together would prove impossible. However, recently American and Israeli scholars have begun to use DNA testing to identify the kind of animal skin each parchment scrap is made from, so that similar fragments can be grouped together and the manuscripts reconstructed. This novel use of a modern scientific technique promises many exciting discoveries in Biblical archeology.

Which places?

What are the reasons for the selection of the places discussed in this volume? Primarily, they are sites that are central to Bible history and have interesting Bible events and stories connected with them. The next important criterion is that there is some linking factor between Bible times and modern times. Some of the towns that feature here are still thriving communities, and have had a continuous existence from then to the present. Others have suffered many vicissitudes, having been destroyed and rebuilt more than once, sometimes on a nearby site. Some – like the once great cities of Babylon, Nineveh, and Ephesus – have simply crumbled away. However, it is still clear where these settlements were located, and archeologists and scholars have often attempted accurate reconstructions of how the cities must once have appeared. Some Bible places were important but were not considered for the book, as their

identity or site is still disputed. Clearly only a small number of the principal places mentioned in the Bible have been covered, but it is hoped that they will give some idea of the rich diversity of the history and geography of Bible lands.

A modern mosaic from a Cypriot monastery shows Jesus as the good shepherd.

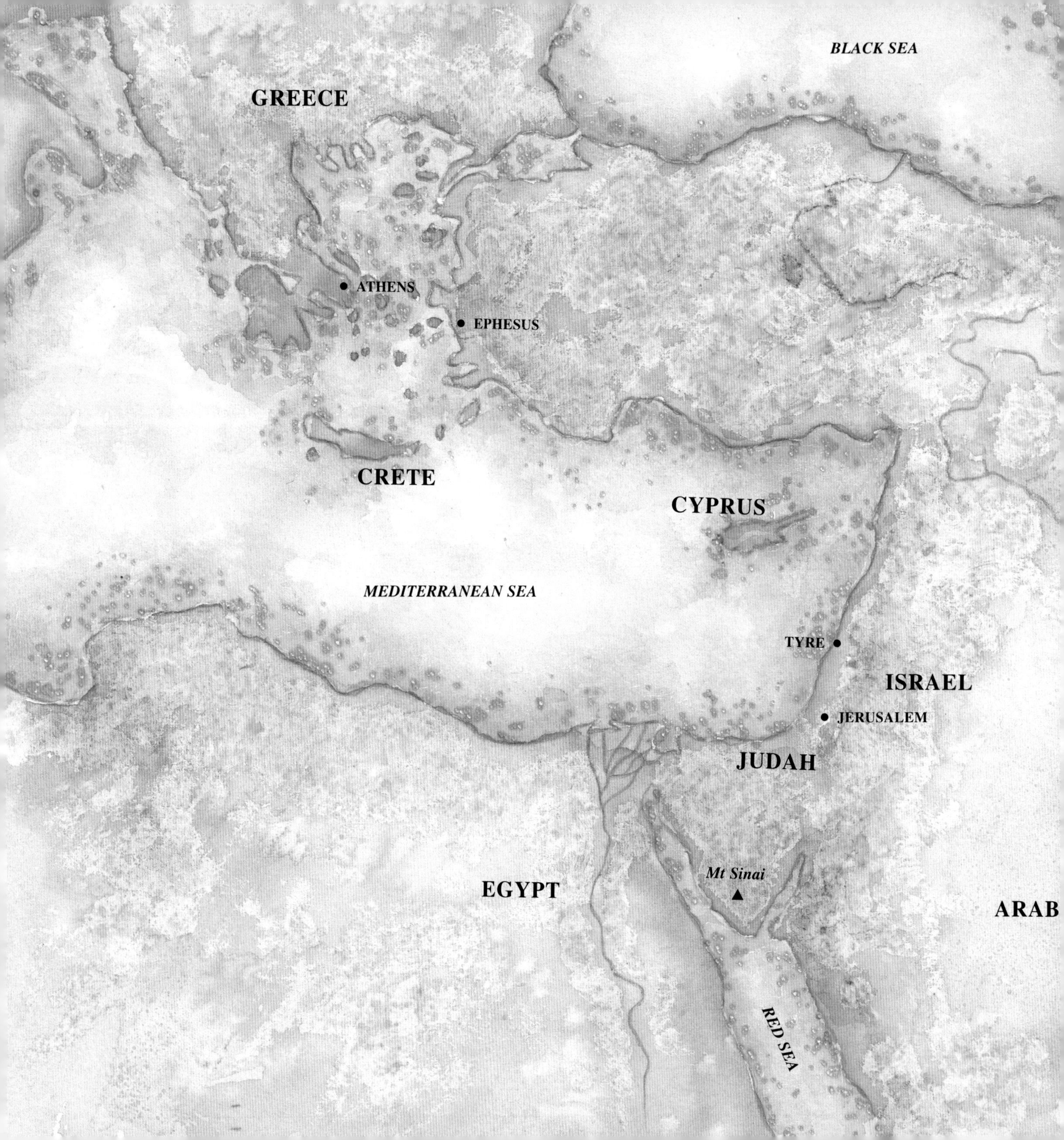

BLACK SEA

GREECE

● ATHENS

● EPHESUS

CRETE

CYPRUS

MEDITERRANEAN SEA

TYRE ●

ISRAEL

● JERUSALEM

JUDAH

EGYPT

Mt Sinai
▲

ARAB

RED SEA

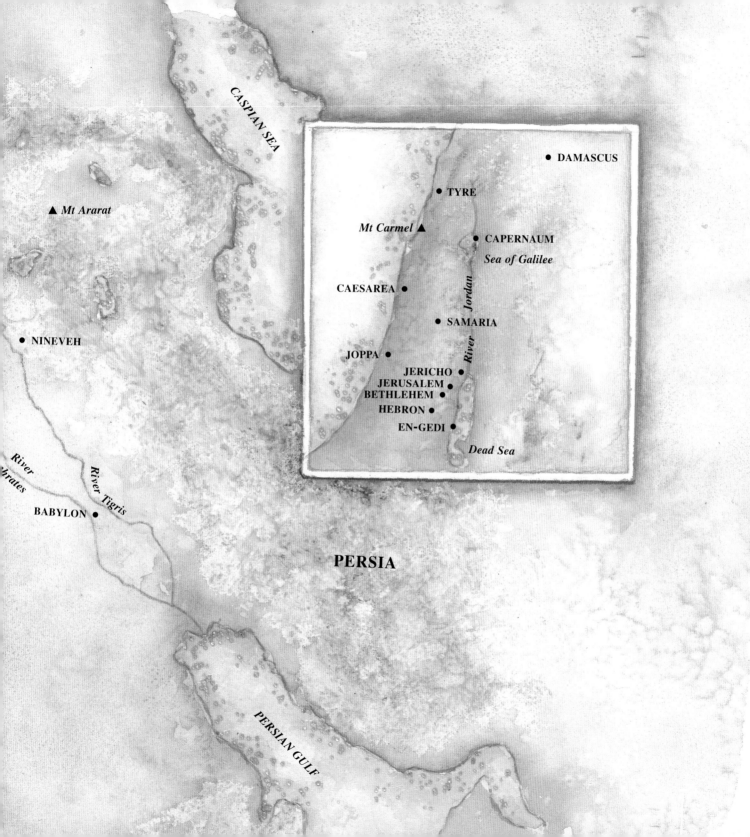

CASPIAN SEA

▲ *Mt Ararat*

• NINEVEH

River Euphrates

River Tigris

BABYLON •

PERSIA

PERSIAN GULF

• DAMASCUS

• TYRE

Mt Carmel ▲

• CAPERNAUM

Sea of Galilee

CAESAREA •

SAMARIA •

Jordan

River

JOPPA •

JERICHO •
JERUSALEM •
BETHLEHEM •

HEBRON •

EN-GEDI •

Dead Sea

BABYLON

The once great city of Babylon, where the Jews were held captive for decades, became a symbol of power, materialism, and cruelty.

The Tower of Babel *by the 16th-century Flemish painter Pieter Brueghel the Elder.*

A 14th-century mosque situated between the city of Baghdad and the site of Babylon.

The city was capital of the ancient land of Babylonia in southern Mesopotamia. It was situated on the River Euphrates 50 miles (80 km) south of modern Baghdad, just north of what is now the modern Iraqi town of al-Hillah.

The Tower of Babel

The name Babylon is a Greek form of the Hebrew name Babel, itself derived from a Sumerian name meaning "Gate of God." Genesis 10:10 describes the founding of the city of Babel by Nimrod, a descendant of Ham, son of Noah. Genesis 11:1–9 describes the building of the city and its famous tower "whose top may reach unto heaven," and how God punished the people's arrogance by creating a confusion of different languages.

Although Babel and Babylon are probably one and the same, there is not sufficient written or archeological evidence to establish that Babel was on the same site as Babylon and, though many have attempted to locate the ruins of the original Tower of Babel, none has succeeded. It is now thought that the legend of the tower refers to a ziggurat built in the 18th century BC.

The growth of Babylon

Although there is some evidence of occupation from prehistoric times, Babylon was not established as a city until the 23rd century BC. It was at first a provincial capital ruled by the kings of the city of Ur, but in the late 19th century BC the Amorite king Sumuabum established a kingdom there. Babylon was enlarged and improved by his successors, particularly Hammurapi, sometimes called Hammurabi (1792–1750 BC),

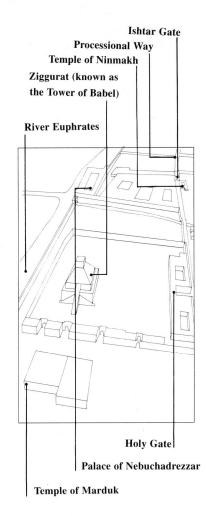

Ishtar Gate

Processional Way

Temple of Ninmakh

Ziggurat (known as
the Tower of Babel)

River Euphrates

Holy Gate

Palace of Nebuchadrezzar

Temple of Marduk

*A reconstruction of
Nebuchadrezzar's great
city, showing a ziggurat
and temples, with the
River Euphrates
flowing through the
middle of the city.*

An illustration from a 19th-century Bible, showing Babylon overwhelmed by the army of Cyrus the Great. The Persian king's army attacked the city in 539 BC.

This hand-tinted illustration of Daniel in the lion's den is taken from an 1816 edition of the John Brown Bible, first published in 1778.

The first six chapters of the Old Testament book of Daniel describe the experiences of Jewish exiles in Babylon after the fall of Jerusalem, when the Jews were taken into captivity.

Daniel was among a group of young men specially chosen from the exiles for their noble birth, intelligence, and good looks, to serve as advisers at the court of King Nebuchadrezzar. They were taught the Babylonian language and instructed in Babylonian literature and philosophy, and were well treated.

The king had a dream which troubled him. He called for all his astrologers and

Part of the remains of Nebudchadrezzar's palace. Iraqi archeologists are reconstructing many of the buildings from the great king's reign.

who enlarged his territory to include many of the neighboring cities, creating a kingdom of Babylonia that stretched over southern Mesopotamia and into Assyria, with Babylon as its capital. It was under his rule that the first ziggurat or Tower of Babel was built. Hammurapi is best known for his Code of Laws, actually not so much a code as a set of legal judgments on 282 different cases, which was inscribed on a stone stela placed in the temple of the god Marduk. Large fragments of this stela were discovered in 1902 by Jean Vincent Scheil in Susa, and it now stands in the Louvre in Paris. The judgments cover economic and family law as well as criminal cases, and are in some ways similar to the Hebrew Mosaic Law.

Under the Amorite dynasty Babylon flourished, but it fell to the Hittites in 1595 BC and then came under control of the Kassites, who established a dynasty that dominated the region for over 400 years, although frequently under foreign attack, particularly from the

Assyrians and the Elamites. In 1158 Babylon was sacked by the Elamites, but soon Elam was conquered by Nebuchadrezzar I, who established a new dynasty in Babylon. This was a time of cultural and literary development when the ancient Babylonian *Epic of Gilgamesh* was rewritten in its finest version.

For several centuries Babylon was a focus of conflict between Assyrian forces and Aramean and Chaldean tribespeople. Assyrian kings dominated from the 9th to the late 7th centuries, and it is with reference to that period that the city is first unequivocally

DANIEL IN BABYLON

fortune tellers and demanded not only that they interpret his dream but that they first describe the dream to him. When none of them could do this Nebuchadrezzar flew into a rage and sentenced all the wise men and royal advisers in Babylon to death; this included Daniel and his companions. Daniel asked for and was granted some more time to interpret the dream. After he had prayed he had a vision which revealed the king's dream. He went to Nebuchadrezzar and described the dream exactly, then interpreted its meaning. The king rewarded Daniel with many gifts and promoted him to his chief adviser.

Daniel was later called upon to interpret another dream for Nebuchadrezzar which put him in a very embarrassing situation, for its meaning would certainly be unwelcome to the king. Nevertheless he boldly told the king that his dream meant that God would punish him for his arrogance by making him insane for seven years. He would be cast out of human society and would live like an animal until he became humble enough to acknowledge God's authority. The king did not heed Daniel but a year later the dream came true.

Daniel continued as adviser under Nebuchadrezzar's son Belshazzar, whose end he prophesied at a great banquet when an invisible hand wrote words on the wall. Daniel told the king that his kingdom would then be divided between the Medes and the Persians. The king was killed the same night, and Darius the Mede became king.

Darius in his turn was impressed by Daniel's wisdom and efficiency. The king's preferential treatment caused resentment, and Daniel's enemies plotted to discredit him. Eventually they persuaded the king to pass a law saying that nobody could make any request to any god or person other than the king, on pain of being cast into a den of lions. They then reported Daniel for contravening the law by regularly praying to God. The king was reluctantly forced to implement the law; Daniel was thrown into a pit filled with lions and the

A stone statue from Babylon representing a lion with a man at its feet. Lions were kept for sport in the royal courts of Mesopotamia.

opening was sealed with a great rock. The next morning Darius came to the lion's den and found that Daniel was completely unharmed. Daniel's accusers were then themselves thrown to the lions, and Darius passed a law commanding that Daniel's God should be respected.

mentioned in the Bible. Hezekiah the King of Judah (716–687 BC) was visited by emissaries from the king of Babylon when he was sick. When he admitted to the prophet Isaiah that he had let these men see the full extent of his wealth, Isaiah prophesied that all the royal treasures would one day be carried off to Babylon (2 Kings 20:12–18). In 689, after a period of nationalist uprisings and unrest in Babylon, the Assyrian king Sennacherib ordered that the city be destroyed. His son Esarhaddon rebuilt it, but the city was badly damaged by fire in 648 during a war between the Assyrian king Ashurbanipal and his brother who ruled over Babylon.

Pride and fall

The decline of the Assyrian empire enabled a Chaldean leader, Nabopolassar, to take control of Babylon in 626 BC. He founded a dynasty which began to restore the damaged city. Under his successor Nebuchadrezzar II (the Nebuchadnezzar of the Bible), who ruled from 605 to 562 BC, Babylon became a great imperial power and the city was splendidly rebuilt, fortified and extended so that it

A Babylonian statue of Ishtar, dating from about 2000 BC. Ishtar – the goddess worshiped in Babylon – was the Mesopotamian form of the Semitic goddess Astarte and was associated both with war and with erotic love.

became the largest city yet seen in the world. The River Euphrates flowed through the middle of the city, though it has since changed its course westwards.

Above: *The half-size reconstruction of the Ishtar Gate built by the Iraq Department of Antiquities at the entrance to the site of ancient Babylon.*
Top: *One of the glazed bricks illustrated with lions, that lined the Processional Way.*

Nebuchadrezzar built or restored palaces and temples, the Processional Way, the Ishtar Gate, and the ziggurat that was known as the Tower of Babel. If the famous Hanging Gardens, one of the Seven Wonders of the World, ever existed, they were built at this time. They may have been a series of terraces covered in trees and plants. Nebuchadrezzar's army conquered Jerusalem, destroyed and plundered the temple, and took the people of Judah back to Babylon as captives (2 Kings 25:1–21). The overweening pride and arrogance of King Nebuchadrezzar is described in the first four chapters of the Book of Daniel.

The despair of the Jewish exiles in Babylon and the prediction of the city's fall are conveyed in several Bible passages, particularly Psalm 137 ("By the rivers of Babylon, there we sat down, yea we wept, when we remembered Zion"); Isaiah 13, 14, 21 ("Babylon is fallen, is fallen," 21:9); and Jeremiah 50–51 ("How is Babylon become a desolation among the nations," 50:23). Daniel 5 describes the death of Nebuchadrezzar's son and successor Belshazzar, when the city was sacked by the Persians under Cyrus in 539. Darius the Mede (Daniel 5:31–6:1–28) was possibly a governor appointed by Cyrus.

Babylon remained under Persian rule for 200 years, diminished in importance but still retaining some of its splendor until the city was destroyed by Xerxes I when he suppressed a rebellion in 482. In 331 BC Alexander the Great conquered Babylon; he had ambitions to rebuild the city and make it his capital, but before he had time to implement his plans he died there in 323. A new city of Seleucia was built on the Tigris and much of Babylon's population moved there in 275 BC. After this Babylon rapidly declined, eventually falling into ruins.

The New Testament mentions Babylon only in reference to the exile of the Jews (Matthew

Enameled bulls and dragons decorate the bricks of the Ishtar Gate.

The Processional Way that led to the Ishtar Gate.

1:17; Acts 7:43) or as a symbol for Rome, which had taken over the role as the great but corrupt oppressor of the people of Israel (Revelation 17:5).

The ruins

Travelers and explorers have been drawn to Babylon for centuries, but serious archeological research did not start until the mid-19th century. Much of the more recent work was carried out by German teams, but in the last few decades the task has been taken over by the Iraqis. Almost all that has been discovered on the site relates to the great city built by King Nebuchadrezzar II. The change in the course of the Euphrates and a rise in the water table, combined with the fact that Nebuchadrezzar rebuilt the city so thoroughly, means that very little from before his time has been found or is likely to be.

Many inscriptions in cuneiform writing, then in general use in Mesopotamia, have been found which describe the city. There is also an account by the Greek historian Herodotus, who visited Babylon in about 460 BC. These make it possible to attempt a reconstruction of Babylon in its prime. There was a vast double wall on both sides of the Euphrates with eight gates, at least one of which, the Ishtar Gate, was faced with glazed bricks depicting bulls and dragons. From the Ishtar Gate ran the Processional Way – a wide paved road flanked by walls decorated with glazed and gilded bricks showing lions and dragons – which led to the temple of Marduk and the adjacent Tower of Babel ziggurat which reached to 300 feet (90 m). There were four other temples, and west of the Ishtar Gate stood two palace complexes. The German archeologist Koldewey, who excavated the site from 1899 to 1917, found vaults in one of these palaces which he identified as the foundations of the legendary Hanging Gardens.

The present site consists of several mounds which cover the remains of Nebuchadrezzar's summer palace, the Ishtar Gate and a further palace complex, the temple of Marduk and the ziggurat, and a residential area. A reconstruction has been made of the Ishtar Gate, and other works of reconstruction and restoration are being carried out by the Iraqis.

The Iraqis continue to reconstruct and restore ancient Babylon. This picture shows the reconstructed city walls.

A series of archways in the reconstructed buildings of Babylon.

THE SEA OF GALILEE

The Sea of Galilee is not a true sea but a large lake in northern Israel. The River Jordan flows through it. The pleasant climate and fertile soil around the lake, and the abundance of fish, made the shores of the Sea of Galilee a desirable place to live, and there is evidence of settlement from prehistoric times. In Jesus' day Galilee was one of the most thriving areas in Israel, its shores dotted with many towns and villages, the most important being Tiberias and Capernaum. Of the nine towns that once flourished there, only Tiberias remains. In the Old Testament the lake is called the Sea of Chinnereth (Numbers 34:11); in the New Testament it is called the Lake of Gennesaret (Luke 5:1) or the Sea of Tiberias (John 21:1), as well as the Sea of Galilee. The modern Hebrew name is Yam Kinneret.

Jesus calls the fishermen

A 14th-century painting by Italian artist Giusto de Giovani de Menabuoi showing the calling of Andrew and Peter from their boat by the Sea of Galilee.

At the start of his ministry Jesus was walking by the shores of the Sea of Galilee. He saw two brothers, Simon (Peter) and Andrew, fishing with nets in the lake. Jesus said to them, "Follow me and I will make you fishers of men." The brothers immediately left their nets and went with Jesus. Jesus continued along the lake until he saw two more fishermen, James and John. They were in a boat with their father Zebedee, mending nets. Jesus called the brothers, who left their boat and followed him (Matthew 4:18–22). In the story told in Luke 5:1–11 Jesus had escaped from the press of people wanting to hear him preach by getting into Simon Peter's boat, rowing out a little way from the land and preaching from the boat. After he had finished preaching, he told Peter to cast his nets into the lake, but Peter answered that there was no point as he had been fishing all night and had caught nothing. However, he obeyed

Jesus and cast his nets. He brought them up with so many fish that the net broke and he had to call for help from James and John. When they returned to the shore, all three of the fishermen left their boats and followed Jesus.

The calming of the storm

Jesus was asleep in a boat with his disciples when a raging storm rose up. His disciples woke him, begging him to save them, and Jesus said to them, "Why are ye fearful, O ye of little faith?" He then stood up and rebuked the wind and the water, saying "Peace, be still," and the lake immediately became calm (Matthew 8:23–27; Mark 4:35–41).

The feeding of the five thousand

At another time a huge crowd again gathered to listen to Jesus speak. Jesus became concerned that the people would be hungry and asked his disciples how such a great number might be fed. Andrew found a boy in the crowd who had five barley loaves and two small fishes but, as he said, "What are they among so many?" Jesus asked his disciples to make the people sit down on the grass. He gave thanks for the food and began to divide it, giving it to his disciples to distribute to the crowd. Not only were all 5,000 people fed, but 12 baskets were filled with the leftovers (John 6:1–14).

Walking on water

Jesus told his disciples to sail over the lake. He then sent the crowd away and went off to a hill to pray, but meanwhile a strong wind had sprung up. Jesus saw his disciples' boat tossing about on the sea and started to walk across the surface of the water to join them. When the disciples saw him they were terrified and thought it was a ghost. Peter said, "Lord, if it be thou, bid me to come unto thee on the water," and Jesus said, "Come." Peter began to walk across the water to Jesus, but as he did so he lost his nerve, and began to sink, crying, "Lord, save me!" Jesus reached out his hand and caught Peter, and they walked back to the boat together (Matthew 14:22–33).

ATHENS

The legacy of centuries of Greek philosophical and religious tradition made the citizens of Athens resistant to Paul's gospel message.

A statue of Athene, the Greek goddess of wisdom who was the patron goddess of Athens and gave her name to the city.

Now capital of modern Greece, Athens is a crowded modern city, housing more than one fourth of Greece's population; but its main attraction still rests in the remains of the architectural wonders of its golden age.

Culture and democracy

The city features in the Book of Acts (17:15–34), and Paul also mentions it in his first letter to the Thessalonians (3:1). A few remains show that Athens was inhabited from Neolithic times, and throughout the Early and Middle Bronze Ages. The earliest buildings date from about 1200 BC, when the Acropolis, the upper part of the city, was first fortified and used as a citadel. The city gradually spread to the northwest. Graves found from this period indicate the prosperity of at least some of the citizens, for they are marked with very large vases richly decorated with pictures of battles and processions.

In the 6th century BC Athens developed considerably: the Acropolis changed its nature from a citadel to a shrine, with a temple devoted to Athene – the goddess of wisdom who gives her name to the city – as well as many smaller shrines and temples. The temple of Athene was built on the site that was later to be occupied by the Parthenon. It was decorated with large sculptures representing lions, bulls, and mythical beasts. A new agora, or market square and general meeting place, was constructed in the lower town.

In 490 BC Greece suffered its first attack from the Persians, who were defeated by the Athenian army at the Battle of Marathon. However, attacks continued and in 480 the city was invaded and destroyed by the Persians. When the Athenians returned to their ruined home the following year, they began a program of rebuilding under their leader

A detail from the porch of the Erechtheum on the Acropolis. Designed by Mnesicles in the 5th century BC, it is one of the finest examples of the use of caryatids, draped female figures used as columns to support a building.

A panoramic view of the city, with a clear view of the Acropolis. The Parthenon is just left of center.

The reconstructed view of the Acropolis in Athen's Golden Age (5th century BC) differs little from that which can be seen by visitors today, if they ignore the vast, crowded city in the background.

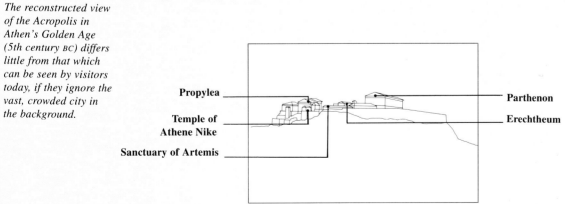

Propylea

Temple of Athene Nike

Sanctuary of Artemis

Parthenon

Erechtheum

The agora, or meeting place. The top picture shows Mars Hill (the Areopagus) in the background; this is where the council originally met. The bottom picture shows the Byzantine-style Church of the Holy Apostles.

Pericles, creating the beautiful city that we associate with the golden age of Athens. Many splendid buildings were constructed in white marble from the nearby Mount Pentelicus, most notably the magnificent Parthenon on the Acropolis, again dedicated to the city's goddess Athene, whose gold and ivory statue stood within the 50 huge columns. Another major work of that period was the Propylea, a huge gateway at the approach to the Acropolis, with five doors and a white marble ceiling. New fortifications and buildings were erected in the lower town. These included the Stoa Poikile, or painted colonnade, in the agora, decorated with paintings including one of the famous Battle of Marathon.

Athens became the leading city of Greece, not only because of its art and architecture, but also in the fields of literature and philosophy. Plato, Aristotle, Epicurus, and Zeno – who founded the Stoic school – all lived and taught in the city. Many writers of the period lived in Athens, including the tragedians Euripides, Aeschylus, and Sophocles; the comic dramatist Aristophanes; and the historian Herodotus, who wrote an account of the city's wars with Persia. The city was also the birthplace of democracy, with all male adult citizens able to vote on matters of both domestic and foreign policy. But the golden age came to an end when Athens lost the Peloponnesian War to the Spartans in 404 BC.

Roman Athens

In the Hellenistic period – the 300 years from 323 BC following the death of Alexander the Great – Athens benefited from building works undertaken by various foreign rulers. The Egyptian Ptolemies built a gymnasium and a sanctuary for the gods Isis and Sarapis. In the 2nd century BC the Attalid rulers of Pergamum built colonnades, one on the slopes of the Acropolis, the other a long building incorporating a row of shops in the agora.

In 86 BC Athens was captured by the Romans. Although there was considerable bloodshed when the city was taken, it was not sacked and the fine public buildings were in general left intact. The invading Romans apparently respected the city's independence and cultural reputation; they allowed it considerable autonomy and erected new buildings. At the time Paul preached there the city had lost its former wealth and power, but remained a center of learning. However, the gospel message was too alien to Greek philosophical and religious thinking to appeal to many Athenians. The passage in Acts 17 which describes Paul's stay in Athens

The remains of the Roman agora. The 1st-century BC Tower of the Winds stands behind what was once a colonnade of shops.

mentions his disputes with philosophers from the Epicurean and Stoic schools. The Epicureans were devoted to the achievement of serenity and happiness through detachment from the desires of the world, and believed that after death the body's constituent particles were dispersed. The Stoics – who took their name from the Stoa Poikile where Zeno had taught – believed primarily in universal reason, and in the disinterested pursuit of virtue and duty. Paul's message might have had some attraction for these philosophers, but his insistence on the idea of resurrection was particularly unacceptable to them. Although some converts were made, and a small Christian community was established, for five or six centuries pagan religion continued to flourish. The Emperor Hadrian completed the temple of Zeus and constructed a library, a Pantheon, and an aqueduct which is still in use.

In AD 267 the Heruli, a Germanic people, briefly captured the city and caused a great deal of damage, destroying all the public buildings of the agora. It was not until the end of the 4th century that Athens began to recover some of its prosperity and to expand again. The city's importance still rested mainly on its academic reputation. When the Emperor Justinian closed the schools of philosophy in 529, Athens lost most of its remaining power; yet it was at this time that Christianity began to be firmly established and many churches were built.

PAUL IN ATHENS

Paul's stay in Athens is described in Acts 17:16–23. Paul did not set out deliberately for Athens, but had to wait there for his companions Silas and Timothy to join him before they went on to Corinth. Paul was distressed to see so much evidence that the city was given over to idolatrous worship. He talked this over with the Jews in the synagogues, and also with various God-fearing Gentiles whom he met in the agora.

Some philosophers from the Stoic and Epicurean schools heard him talking and were interested to know what new doctrine he was propounding. They asked him to go to the Areopagus, a council named for the Hill of Mars (Ares in Greek) but which probably now met at the "Royal Porch" in the agora. They were sure that others would want to hear this new message.

Paul addressed the council, saying that he had noticed how religious the citizens of Athens were, for he had seen so many temples, statues, and altars dedicated to various gods, including one altar inscribed "To the Unknown God." He declared that he would make this God known to them, for God is the creator of all things, and does not reside in statues and temples. The gold and silver and stone images that they worshiped had nothing to do with God's true nature, and the time had now come when God did not excuse their ignorance but demanded repentance and true worship. A day of judgment was

This picture of Paul preaching at Athens is one of the cartoons painted by the great Italian Renaissance artist Raphael for the tapestries in the Sistine Chapel in Rome.

coming; God had chosen the man who would judge the world, and had proved his ordination for the task by raising him from the dead.

This talk of resurrection was too much for most of Paul's hearers, who mocked him, but others were more interested and a small group – including one Dionysius, who was a member of the council – accepted his message and joined him.

Occupation and freedom

Athens continued to decline, from a provincial city of the Byzantine empire, to a Crusader stronghold and then, in the middle of the 15th century, a Turkish possession. The Parthenon in turn became an Orthodox cathedral in Byzantine times, then a Catholic one under the Crusaders, and under the Turks a mosque, with the addition of a minaret. Apart from a period in 1687 when Athens was taken by the Venetians, the city remained under Turkish rule for over 400 years. During the war with the Venetians ammunition was stored in the Parthenon, part of which was destroyed when the powder exploded.

By the time Greece finally achieved its independence, with Athens becoming its capital in 1833, the city's population had shrunk to little more than 4,000. The Turks had destroyed much of the ancient city and sold off various works of art to Europeans, including the famous Elgin marbles. These were sculptures taken from the Parthenon and other parts of the Acropolis in 1801 by the British ambassador Lord Elgin, who then sold them to the British Museum.

The new King of the Hellenes, Otto, was a Bavarian, and German architects took over the rebuilding of the city in their idea of a neo-Grecian style. All remains of the long Turkish occupation were destroyed, and work began on reconstructing what remained of the ancient city. The population gradually rose, with a sudden dramatic increase after World War I, when the city began to become seriously overpopulated, and spread out in new suburbs and urban slums.

Two archeological treasures of Athens from the 15th–16th centuries BC. The gold mask comes from the tombs of Mycenae, excavated in the 1870s. The golden cup was found in the "beehive" tomb at Vaphio, excavated in 1889, and depicts a pastoral scene.

Athens suffered greatly during the German occupation in World War II, when many of the inhabitants starved to death and the fabric of the city crumbled. After the war things did not improve, for civil war broke out. Once peace returned to Athens, work began on constructing new buildings, and on the preservation of the ruins of ancient Athens. New apartment buildings sprang up everywhere as the population continued to increase and the city boundaries to spread. Growing industrialization and the ever-increasing traffic in the city led to a new problem: severe air pollution. Although Athens still attracts huge numbers of tourists, its overcrowding and the infamous smog make it a less attractive city than formerly.

This print from about 1885 shows a reconstruction of ancient Athens.

The remains of the Parthenon, built between 447 and 438 BC and still the most impressive building in Athens.

The theater of Herodes Atticus. It was first built in AD 161 by a rich Roman, Herodes Atticus, as a memorial to his wife. Now without its roof, it is still used as a theater for summer festivals.

Remains of ancient Athens

For the visitor to Athens the chief attraction is probably still the Parthenon, which remains extraordinarily impressive despite the depredations of the years. There is not a single straight line in its construction; everything is slightly curved to achieve perfect proportion and harmony.

The other major sight on the Acropolis is the great entry gate, the Propylea. The temple of Athene Nike stood to the right of the Propylea. Destroyed by the Turks, it was restored in 1836 but in the 1930s its foundations started to crumble, and work on them revealed the remains of an earlier temple on the site, dating from the 6th century BC and dedicated to Artemis.

On the slopes of the Acropolis is the odeum, or theater, built in AD 161 to seat 5,000 spectators. The semicircular auditorium is carved out of the rock of the hill itself. Its original cedar roof has disappeared, but it is still used as an open-air theater. Nearby are the ruins of the much older Dionysiac theater where drama competitions were held. The prizes were displayed in monuments that stood near the theater, and one of these has survived.

The agora has undergone restoration since the 1930s, when the area was cleared of the housing that had accumulated, and a museum was built in a reconstruction of the 2nd century colonnade built by Attalus. The Theseum near the agora, a temple of the 5th century, is the only building from the golden age that has remained almost intact, though it lacks the simple beauty of the Parthenon.

This view of the city shows modern buildings in the foreground, with the ancient buildings of the Acropolis visible in the background.

HEBRON

The troubled town of Hebron has seen one rebellion after another – against the Gibeonites and Joshua, against King David, against the British mandate, and most recently as a center of the intifada *against the Israelis.*

The burial place of Isaac and his wife Rebecca in the Tombs of the Patriarchs in Hebron.

ebron is the highest town in Palestine, 19 miles (30 km) southwest of Jerusalem, and 3,050 feet (930 m) above sea level. It has many Old Testament associations, and the modern town on the west bank of the Jordan is a holy place for both Muslims and Jews.

The patriarch's burial place

Hebron is one of the few places whose origin is clearly dated in the Bible. In Numbers 13:22 the town is stated to have been "built seven years before Zoan in Egypt." Zoan, later known as Tanis, is thought to date from about 1720 BC.

The first reference to Hebron in the Bible is in connection with Abraham setting up his tent at nearby Mamre (Genesis 13:18). When Hebron is next mentioned in Genesis 23 it is also given its alternative name of Karjath-arba (or Kiriath Arba in some versions), which means "city of four." The significance of this is obscure, but it might refer to four settlements in the area. The passage relates how Abraham's wife Sarah died at Hebron, and how Abraham negotiated with the local Hittite people to buy the field of Machpelah, so that he could bury her in the cave there and keep it as a family burial place. Abraham in his turn was buried in the cave at Hebron (Genesis 25:8–10), as were his son Isaac

(Genesis 35:27), Isaac's wife Rebekah, their son Jacob and his wife Leah (Genesis 49:29–31, 50:13).

A town of giants

When Moses, having led the people of Israel out of Egypt to wander in the wilderness, sent out spies to reconnoiter the land of Canaan,

The modern town of Hebron, scene of much unrest in the Arab–Israeli conflict.

Part of the Herodian construction at Machpelah, site of the Patriarchs' burial places, and now occupied by a mosque. The cutaway section shows the original cave where Abraham and Sarah are buried.

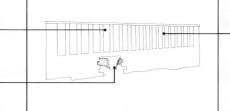

Haram al-Khalil (Arabic name for the Tomb of the Patriarchs)

Cave of Machpelah (which translates as double cave)

Herodian enclosure (built over cave)

The tomb of Sarah in the mosque at Hebron.

they went to Hebron. They brought back with them grapes from the "brook of Eshcol." The name derives from the Hebrew for a bunch of grapes, and the vineyards around Hebron still produce fine quality grapes. The spies also complained that Hebron was inhabited by "giants," the people of Anak, who were renowned for their exceptional stature (Numbers 13).

After the Israelites under Joshua had conquered Canaan, war broke out against the people of Gibeon, who had made peace with Joshua. Hoham, king of Hebron, joined the alliance of leaders warring against Gibeon, and was killed by Joshua (Joshua 10:1–26). Later Joshua gave Hebron to Caleb, one of the spies who had first reported on Canaan; he and Joshua had been the only ones to have displayed courage and urged the people to go in and take the land. Caleb was presented with Hebron as an inheritance for his family, and he drove out the people of Anak (14:13–15, 15:13–14).

Hebron is next heard of in 2 Samuel, which recounts events starting just after the death of King Saul in about 1000 BC. God commanded David to go to Hebron, and he was anointed king of Judah there (2:1–4), and later king of Israel too. He reigned from Hebron for seven and a half years before he conquered Jerusalem and made it his capital (5:1–5).

Solomon's son Rehoboam fortified Hebron (2 Chronicles 11:10). It was during his reign that the kingdom divided, with the northern tribes forming the separate kingdom of Israel. There is evidence that Hebron was still an important royal town in the southern kingdom of Judah during Hezekiah's reign (716–687 BC), from inscriptions mentioning the city on jar handles from that period. After the Babylonian exile, Hebron was re-populated by the returning Jews (Nehemiah 11:25), but subsequently it fell to the Edomites, from whom it was taken by Judas Maccabeus, as related in the apocryphal book of 1 Maccabees (5:65).

Al-Khalil

Herod the Great built a wall around the cave of Machpelah, some of which still stands. The city was burnt by the Romans when it was occupied by Jewish rebels in AD 66–70. It first came under Muslim rule in 635 and, apart from a period of Crusader rule from 1100 to 1260, it remained so until after World War I, by which time a small Jewish community coexisted with the Arab Muslim majority. The town's Arab name is al-Khalil or, in full, al-Khalil ar-Rahman (the beloved of merciful God, namely Abraham).

The first building housing the tombs of the patriarchs dates from the Byzantine period. In 1115 the Crusaders built a church within Herod's wall. Augustinian friars constructed a stairway down into a narrow rock-cut passage that led to the cave, where they discovered bones. The present mosque is a rebuilding of the Crusader church. The cenotaphs of Abraham and Sarah stand in two octagonal chapels at the north and south ends of the mosque. There is a small window near Abraham's cenotaph with a stone said to carry the mark of Adam's foot.

From 1923 to 1948 Hebron came under the British mandate. During that period there were several Arab uprisings, and Hebron's

Part of the original 12th-century Crusader church built to shelter the Tombs of the Patriarchs.

ABSALOM'S REBELLION

Absalom was King David's third son, a very beautiful, long-haired young man. He was much loved by David but had fled from his father's wrath after having organized the murder of Amnon, David's first son, as revenge for Amnon having raped his half-sister, Absalom's full sister Tamar (2 Samuel 13).

Eventually David forgave Absalom, and father and son were reconciled (2 Samuel 14). But Absalom began to seek power for himself. After four years (40 in some versions) he asked David for permission to go to Hebron, to fulfill a vow that if he was allowed to return to Jerusalem he would go and worship the Lord at Hebron, which was considered a sanctified place because of the patriarchs who were buried there. Absalom left Jerusalem for Hebron with a retinue of 200 men. From this base he began plotting rebellion against his father. Word got to David of the rebellion that his son was brewing, and he fled from Jerusalem (2 Samuel 15:1–14).

The story inevitably ended sadly: David was forced into battle with Absalom and his followers, although he told his commanders to "deal gently for my sake with . . . Absalom." However, Absalom was caught by his long hair in a tree, where David's men killed him. David mourned him bitterly, crying: "Would God I had died for thee, O Absalom, my son, my son!" (2 Samuel 18).

This French engraving illustrates 2 Samuel 18:9–15; Absalom is caught in an oak tree by his long hair, and is killed by David's men.

Jews were either killed or left the city. After 1949 Hebron became part of Jordan, but after the war of 1967 it became part of the occupied West Bank, and Jewish settlers moved in. The September 1995 peace agreement placed it under Palestinian control, but with Israeli army protection for the Jewish settlers. Much of the mosque has been turned into a museum but parts of it remain open for worship to both Jews and Muslims, and it attracts many pilgrims. Another focus for tourists is Abraham's Oak, at the site supposed to be Mamre, about a mile (1.6 km) from the town of Hebron, and under the control of the Russian Orthodox Church.

Market stalls in Hebron, in front of the Mosque of Abraham.

THE PHILISTINES

The Philistine people, who probably originated in the Aegean, settled in southern Canaan in the 12th or 13th century BC, before the Israelites arrived. They inhabited the cities of Gath, Gaza, Ashdod, Ashkelon, and Ekron. This area was known as Philistia, a name which later became Palestine. The Philistines adopted the language, culture, and religion of Canaan, although there is evidence of a distinctive Philistine culture, notably in pottery and ironworking.

Samson and the Philistines

Samson was born at a time when the Philistines ruled over the Israelites. Before his birth an angel told his mother that the son she was to bear would be dedicated to God and would begin the liberation of the people from the Philistines. He was to touch no alcohol, and his hair must never be cut.

Samson grew up an extraordinarily strong young man but he had one weakness: a liking for Philistine women. He fell in love with a Philistine girl and wanted to marry her. Samson set a riddle to the 30 young Philistine men who attended the wedding feast, betting each one a suit of clothes that he could not solve it. The Philistines found out the answer by setting Samson's bride to nag him until he told her. When they told him the answer Samson, knowing that he had been tricked, killed 30 Philistine men at random, took their clothes, and gave them to the men who had answered the riddle. But he deserted his deceitful wife and her father gave her to another man. Samson took revenge for this by catching 300 foxes, tying firebrands to their tails, and turning them loose in the Philistines' fields to destroy all their crops.

The Philistines began to attack the people of Judah, who discovered that it was Samson that they wanted, so they took him prisoner and prepared to hand him over to their enemies. But Samson broke his bonds, seized the jawbone of a dead ass and killed a thousand Philistines with it. After this he became a "judge" or chieftain in Judah for 20 years.

Samson met a Philistine prostitute in Gaza. While he was in bed with her the townspeople plotted to kill him at daybreak. But Samson rose at midnight and pulled down the city gate and walked off with it.

The next woman he fell in love with was Delilah. The kings of the five Philistine towns bribed her to discover the secret of his strength. Three times Samson lied to her, but eventually he admitted that if his hair was cut he would lose his strength. Delilah lulled him to sleep in her arms and then called the Philistines, who cut off his hair. Samson's strength had left him so he was powerless as the Philistines put out his eyes, chained him, and imprisoned him in Gaza. The Philistine kings met at Gaza for a great celebration and called for Samson to be brought in to entertain them. But Samson's hair had grown while he was in prison. He stood between two pillars, took hold of them, and pushed with all his strength. The building collapsed, killing Samson and all the Philistines there (Judges 13–16).

David and Goliath

When Saul became the first king of Israel his army was engaged in constant battle with the Philistines. The Philistines sent one of their soldiers, Goliath, to challenge the Israelites to single combat. He was an enormous man from Gath, said to be over 9 feet (3 m) tall.

David holding the head of the Philistine warrior Goliath; the picture is by the 16th-century Italian painter Caravaggio.

David was the youngest son of Jesse from Bethlehem; three of his older brothers were in Saul's army, but David tended his father's sheep. One day Jesse sent David to the camp with food for the soldiers, and to see how his brothers were faring. David saw Goliath come out once again to challenge the Israelites and volunteered to fight him. The king eventually agreed and gave David his own armor but it was much too heavy for the boy, so he took it off. He found five smooth stones to cast with his sling, and armed with these and his shepherd's stick he went out to face Goliath. Goliath mocked the boy, but David told him that he came against him in the name of God. He launched a stone at Goliath with his sling and it hit the giant's forehead, breaking his skull and killing him (1 Samuel 17).

BETHLEHEM

*Known principally as the birthplace of Jesus, Bethlehem
also has many significant links with the Old Testament.*

*Rachel's tomb, in
what is now the
Arab cemetery. Rachel
died near Bethlehem
after giving birth
to Benjamin.*

The small town of Bethlehem lies in the Judean hills about 5 miles (8 km) south of Jerusalem. It is now an independent Palestinian-controlled township, and is a busy center of agriculture and trade, and a magnet for tourists and pilgrims who flock to it as the site of the birth of Jesus. The name means "the house of bread;" in Arabic it is Bayt Lahm.

Royal David's city

The first mention of Bethlehem is in the book of Genesis, for it was nearby that Rachel, Jacob's wife, died giving birth to her son Benjamin, and was buried (35:16–20). The town is referred to both by its older name of Ephrath and as Bethlehem. It was sometimes called Bethlehem Ephrathah or Bethlehem Judah, to distinguish it from another Bethlehem that lay northwest of Nazareth.

Bethlehem appears in the Old Testament book of Ruth, which was probably written in the late 5th or the 4th century BC. This describes how a family from Bethlehem traveled to Moab to escape famine in Judah. The husband and two sons died in Moab, but the widowed Naomi returned to her homeland, accompanied by her Moabite daughter-in-law Ruth, who refused to leave her and vowed to adopt Naomi's religion and people as her own. When they returned to Bethlehem Ruth started to work as a reaper in the fields of Naomi's rich kinsman Boaz, who eventually married her. The last few verses are a genealogy which shows that Ruth and Boaz were the great-grandparents of David.

Ruth's descendants apparently remained in Bethlehem, for when the prophet Samuel was sent to anoint a king over Israel to be Saul's successor, God told him to choose one of the sons of Jesse the Bethlehemite, Ruth's grandson (1 Samuel 16:1). Samuel traveled to Bethlehem where God directed him to choose David, the youngest son, a boy who spent his days looking after his father's sheep in the hills outside Bethlehem. After David became king, during the continuing wars with the Philistines, Bethlehem became a Philistine garrison town, and three of David's "mighty men" risked their lives to fetch water from the well by the city gate of Bethlehem, because David had a longing for water from that well

*Engraving of a pastoral
scene, with the Church
of the Nativity in the
background.*

*One of the 10th-century
Crusader mosaics from
the Church of the
Nativity.*

44

Justinian's 6th-century Church of the Nativity stands among the vines and olive trees of the village. The square stone watch towers can still be seen on the outskirts of the modern town.

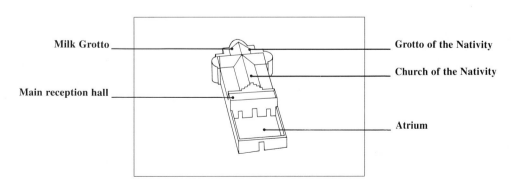

Milk Grotto

Main reception hall

Grotto of the Nativity

Church of the Nativity

Atrium

The caldarium, or hot bath, at the Herodium, Herod's winter palace near Bethlehem, with the ceiling of the frigidarium, or cold bath, inset. The Roman fashion was to proceed through a series of hot and cold baths and steam rooms, interspersed with anointing and exercise, and finish up in the swimming pool.

(2 Samuel 23:15–17). Although David reigned as king in Jerusalem, which was known as "the City of David," Bethlehem established a vital claim to that title, as the place of David's birth and boyhood.

After the division of the kingdom, Bethlehem was one of the towns that were fortified by Rehoboam, David's grandson and the first king of Judah (2 Chronicles 11:5–6). In common with the other towns near Jerusalem, Bethlehem was attacked by Nebuchadrezzar and laid waste; it was repopulated only when the Jewish people returned from captivity in Babylon.

The last mention of Bethlehem in the Old Testament comes in one of the minor prophets, Micah, who prophesies, "But thou, O Bethlehem Ephrathah . . . out of thee shall he come forth unto me that is to be ruler in Israel" (5:2).

The place of the Nativity

The story of Jesus' birth in Bethlehem is told in just two of the Gospels, Matthew and Luke. It was important to establish Bethlehem as the birthplace of Christ, mainly because of Micah's Messianic prophecy, but also because it connected Jesus with David, as the Old Testament prophets believed that the Messiah would come from the house of David. In fact it is Joseph rather than Mary who is represented as a descendant of David, which presents some problems for those who insist both on Jesus' direct descent from David and on the doctrine of the virgin birth.

In Matthew's Gospel there is no explanation of why Jesus happened to be born in Bethlehem, and it could be assumed that Mary and Joseph were already living in the town. However, Luke's Gospel tells the familiar story of Mary and Joseph traveling from Nazareth to Bethlehem in order to be "enrolled" – that is, registered and taxed. Matthew's story describes how Herod sought to destroy the child; how Mary, Joseph, and the baby fled to Egypt to evade him; how Herod then had all the male babies in Bethlehem killed; and how the family returned to Israel after Herod's death. This

The Herodium, the hill where Herod built his palace. Although it was primarily a pleasure palace with swimming pool and gardens, it was also heavily fortified.

CHRIST IS BORN IN BETHLEHEM

The Adoration of the Shepherds, *by the 17th-century French painter Nicolas Poussin.*

The Gospel of Luke (2:1–20) describes how Augustus issued a decree which compelled all the people to go to their own cities to be enrolled for the census. As Joseph was descended from David he had to travel from his home town of Nazareth to Bethlehem, taking with him his betrothed wife, Mary, who was pregnant. While they were in Bethlehem, Mary's labor started and she gave birth to a son. She wrapped him in swaddling clothes and laid him in a manger, because there was no room for them in the inn.

That night, in the fields outside Bethlehem, shepherds were watching their sheep. An angel appeared to them and, telling them not to be afraid, announced the good news: the Savior Christ, the Messiah, had been born that day in Bethlehem. They would find him wrapped in swaddling clothes and lying in a manger. Then a whole host of angels appeared, praising God. The shepherds hurried to the town where they found Mary and Joseph, with the baby lying in the manger as the angels had described.

The Magi of the Christmas story appear in Matthew's version (2:1–18), which describes how wise men came from the East to Jerusalem seeking the child who was to be king of the Jews, for they had seen his star in the East and wanted to worship him. The Gospel does not say that there were three of them or that they were kings, as later tradition held. Probably they were astrologers, perhaps from Arabia or Babylon. When Herod heard of their quest he asked his priests where they expected the Messiah to be born; they cited the prophecy from Micah mentioning Bethlehem. Herod then sent the wise men to Bethlehem to find the child and report back to him. Guided by the same star that they had seen in the East, the wise men came to Bethlehem and found the baby Jesus. They worshiped him and gave him gifts of gold, frankincense, and myrrh.

Warned in a dream not to return to Herod, the wise men went back to their own country. Joseph too had a dream in which an angel told him to flee to Egypt with his family as Herod would seek to destroy the child. They immediately left for Egypt. Herod, when he found that the wise men were not going to return, had all the male children in Bethlehem who were under two years old killed.

This Nativity picture is taken from a richly decorated 15th-century Book of Hours.

The silver star in the grotto of the Church of the Nativity; it is believed to mark the actual spot where Jesus was born.

link with the last years of Herod I seems to establish Jesus' birth as 4 BC but Luke's account, linking the birth with the first census organized by Augustus Caesar, puts it at 6 BC.

Bethlehem was not an obscure village at the time of Jesus' birth, as it is often represented. It was near the busy main road from Jerusalem to Gaza via Hebron, and so much visited by travelers. It was also close to the site of the Herodium, a conical hill where Herod had built a combined fortress and pleasure palace, with a swimming pool and formal gardens.

Later history

In AD 131, when Israel was under the Emperor Hadrian, a Jewish leader called Bar Kokhba led a revolt against the Romans. In reprisal, Bethlehem was made a Roman garrison town and all the Jews were expelled. Hadrian apparently planted a grove of trees sacred to Adonis around the cave that had been identified as the site of the Nativity. It was not until Constantine I's reign 200 years later that this grove was destroyed and a church built over the site by Helena, Constantine's mother, who was converted to Christianity before her son and is said to have found the remains of the cross on which Jesus was crucified. Helena's church at Bethlehem was rebuilt as the present Church of the Nativity in the 6th century by the Emperor Justinian. In 386 St Jerome settled in Bethlehem and built a monastery. Here he translated the Old and

New Testaments into Latin, producing the "Vulgate" (popular) version that is still used by the Roman Catholic Church.

Bethlehem has remained a monastic town and center for pilgrimage for centuries, but its peace has often been disturbed. In 1847 the silver star on the floor of the Church of the Nativity, that was supposed to mark the spot where Jesus was born, was stolen, starting a dispute that led indirectly to the Crimean War. From 1923 to 1948 the town was part of the British mandate over Palestine. It became part of Jordan in 1950 and from 1967 to 1995 was part of the Israeli-occupied West Bank. During the recent *intifada*, or anti-Israeli uprising, riots and violent demonstrations in Bethlehem's Manger Square became a regular feature at Christmas, often preventing pilgrims from joining in the traditional processions. Under the September 1995 peace accord, it came under Palestinian control.

Below: *The Milk Grotto, where the infant Jesus is supposed to have been nursed by Mary.* **Bottom:** *The Christmas procession in Manger Square outside the Church of the Nativity.*

Engraving of the grotto of the Nativity, showing the steps leading down to the cave with its silver lamps and star.

Bethlehem today

The modern town of Bethlehem is not just a place of tourism but a working agricultural market town. It is home to many convents and monasteries, as well as churches of all denominations. There is a traditional trade in the manufacture of religious goods made from mother-of-pearl.

The Church of the Nativity is, of course, the greatest tourist attraction. It is in the joint hands of the Roman Catholic and the Greek and Armenian Orthodox Churches, and priests from all three denominations preside there. Very little changed from the time of its rebuilding by Justinian, the church is one of the oldest in existence, although there have naturally been many repairs and later additions over the centuries. The walled-in arch at the one small entrance dates from the time of the Crusades, and there are many medieval frescos in the various chapels. The Grotto of the Nativity is entered by flights of steps on each side of the choir; it is a small, dark cave lit by silver lamps, its rough limestone walls still visible behind marble slabs and tapestry.

Another attraction, situated close by the Church of the Nativity, is the Milk Grotto, traditionally the site where Mary nursed the infant Jesus. It is a cave decorated with carvings and statues, most of them representing the Virgin and Child. A tradition has grown of pilgrims taking away small pieces of the cave's soft chalk to grind and feed to nursing mothers.

In some ways the town has hardly altered over the centuries. In the hills around the town nomadic Arabs set up their tents and shepherds watch their flocks, like the boy David and also the shepherds of the Christmas story. The approach to Bethlehem is along a dusty road lined with stone terraces planted mainly with olive trees. The traveler's first view of the town is of flat-roofed white houses clustered together on a hillside. Many old houses in the town are built over caves cut into the limestone. The caves are level with the road and a flight of rough steps leads up to the one-room houses where the family lives. The caves, housing animals and mangers, or stone troughs, are often cut into the rock. It was probably in just such a cave that Jesus was born, rather than the barnlike stable that most of us imagine today.

Below: *An ageless scene of an Arab on his donkey outside Bethlehem.*
Bottom: *A typical street in the city.*

Lost Treasures of the Old Testament

I n the early pioneering days of Biblical
archeology, many scholars set off to the Bible
lands hoping to find some of the treasures referred to
in the Old Testament. Usually they were disappointed,
because it was impossible to locate sites accurately,
and because so many artifacts have rotted or been
otherwise destroyed. As archeological techniques have
progressed some impressive treasures have been
discovered, but many others remain elusive.

Noah's Ark
One of the best-loved Bible stories
tells how God instructed Noah to
build an ark so that he, his family,
and representatives of all the
animals, could be saved from the
imminent flood (Genesis 6–8).
Noah built the ark to God's
specifications and after the flood
the ark came to rest on Mount
Ararat. For years travelers and
archeologists have searched
the Ararat mountain range
for traces of Noah's ark. Pieces
of wood have been found, and
recently a large boat-shaped
depression in the rocks was
discovered. However, no hard
scientific evidence can be cited
to link these findings with the
ancient story.

*Illustration from a 15th-century
Book of Hours manuscript showing
the building of Noah's ark.*

The Ark of the Covenant

The Ark of the Covenant was an elaborately decorated chest, with poles to make it portable, intended both as a receptacle for the tablets of the Law and as a sanctuary for God (Exodus 25:9–22). It was carried by the Israelites throughout their wanderings and did not find a permanent home until Solomon placed it in his temple (1 Kings 8:1–21). As there was no Ark in the second temple, one can assume that it was lost, stolen, or destroyed when Jerusalem fell to the Babylonians in 587 BC. Scholars have found evidence of shrines in the form of boxes made of wood and gold, dating from before Moses' time, but the Ark itself remains a lost treasure.

The Ark of the Covenant, as depicted in an English manuscript promoting Christian knowledge in 1817.

Archeologists hope to unlock the secret of the balsam oil using samples scraped from the vats and oil jars found in En-Gedi.

The Secret of En-Gedi

The Dead Sea oasis of En-Gedi is often mentioned in the Old Testament and was famed for the aromatic plants that grew there (Song of Solomon 1:14). Excavations in 1971 unearthed a splendid synagogue, with a mosaic floor inscribed with a curse on he "who reveals the secret of the village to the Gentiles." In 1996 archeologists discovered a buried village, abandoned for 14 centuries, which contains a factory for the manufacture of the precious balsam oil used for the anointing of the kings of Judah. Ancient historians have recorded that this oil was produced at En-Gedi in the 6th century BC.

DAMASCUS

*Damascus, a city frequently mentioned in the
Old Testament, was also the scene of the dramatic
conversion of St Paul.*

*Damascus' famous
Straight Street, showing
the East Gate.*

*A view of the city, with
the Qāsiyūn Mountain
(Jabal Qāsiyūn) in the
background and the
Church of Qāsiyūn in
the foreground.
The city's expansion
has pushed much
residential housing
up the slopes of
Jabal Qāsiyūn.*

Capital of Syria since antiquity, Damascus was a center for trade and communications in Old and New Testament times, and remains a hub of commerce and industry. Its Arabic name is Dimashq, or sometimes ash-Sham. The city is situated east of the Anti-Lebanon Mountains on the River Barada 50 miles (80 km) from the Mediterranean, and surrounded by an oasis.

An Aramean kingdom

The earliest evidence of settlement in Damascus is pottery that dates from the third millennium BC, but the city is probably older still. By the second millennium it had become a significant city and the final destination for the King's Highway trading route from the Gulf of Aqaba, which was used between the 23rd and 20th centuries BC and again between the 13th and the 6th. Damascus is first mentioned in the Bible in a story about Abraham pursuing some kings who had captured his nephew Lot (Genesis 14:15), and then as the home of Abraham's steward Eliezer (Genesis 15:2).

Damascus grew in importance as the capital city of Aram and home of the Aramean people who dominated the area between the 11th and 8th centuries BC. Aram and Aramean are translated as "Syria" and "Syrian" in the King James and some other English versions of the Old Testament; but this is not really accurate, as Syria did not exist as such at that time. The Arameans were originally a semi-nomadic Semitic people who gradually infiltrated the Mesopotamian and Syrian areas over several centuries and eventually established the area around Damascus as their principal stronghold. They worshiped Baal, Hadad (or Rimmon) the storm god, and a fertility goddess identified with Astarte. One part of their culture had an

The gateway to Straight Street, the street in Damascus that is mentioned in the New Testament book of Acts, and in the modern town remains a busy thoroughfare lined with small shops and stores.

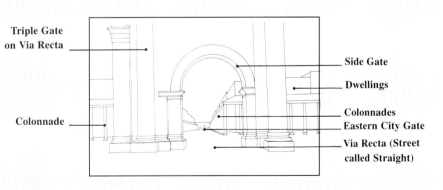

Triple Gate on Via Recta

Side Gate

Dwellings

Colonnade

Colonnades

Eastern City Gate

Via Recta (Street called Straight)

ELISHA AND NAAMAN

The story of Naaman, the Damascene army commander, is told in 2 Kings 5. Naaman was a very successful officer but suffered from leprosy (or more likely some other serious skin disease). A young Israelite girl who had been taken as a prisoner of war and was working as a maidservant for Naaman's wife remarked to her mistress that Naaman could be healed if he went to see the prophet who lived in Samaria.

Naaman informed the king of Syria what the girl had said, and the king sent Naaman to the king of Israel with a letter asking him to ensure that the commander was healed. The king of Israel – probably Jehoram, Ahab's son – was distraught when he read this, for he had no idea how the man could be healed and assumed that this was a ploy by the king of Syria to start a dispute with him. However, word reached Elisha of what was happening and he sent a message to the king, advising him to send the commander on to him.

Naaman went to Elisha's house, where the prophet sent a servant to meet him and give him instructions to wash himself seven times in the River Jordan in order to be healed. Naaman went away in disgust, furious that the prophet had not bothered to come out and heal him personally and unable to believe that the Jordan could

A picture of the prophet Elisha, taken from a Victorian bible.

have any qualities superior to those of the Damascene rivers Abana (Barada) and Pharpar (Awaj). But he was persuaded by his servants to do as Elisha had said: he washed himself seven times in the Jordan and found that his skin had become perfectly clear.

Naaman returned to Elisha and declared that his healing had convinced him that there was no god but the God of Israel. He tried to insist on giving Elisha a valuable present but the prophet would not accept any reward. However, Elisha had a servant, Gehazi, who witnessed this and thought his master very foolish to refuse Naaman's offer. Gehazi decided that he could profit from the Damascene's healing. He pursued Naaman's chariot and pretended that he carried a message from his master saying that two prophets had just arrived to see him and he would like a talent of silver (3,000 pieces) and some clothes for them. Naaman graciously gave Gehazi two talents of silver and some fine clothes. When Gehazi returned he hid the gifts and lied when Elisha questioned him as to where he had been. But Elisha knew what Gehazi had done and prophesied that the servant – and all his descendants – would be struck with leprosy. And immediately Gehazi's skin became "as white as snow."

Straight Street, mentioned in Acts 9:11 as the street where Paul stayed after his conversion.

important influence over the Hebrew people – their language, Aramaic. First it was used in trade and diplomacy, then it became a lingua franca over the whole of the Near East. By the 9th century BC it had largely replaced Hebrew as the language of the Israelite people. Parts of the Old Testament books of Ezra and Daniel were written in Aramaic, and it was the language that Jesus spoke.

The Aramean kings of Damascus were often under attack, and were conquered by King David, who captured and garrisoned Damascus after its people had come to the aid of Hadadezer, the king from the neighboring Aramean town of Zobah (2 Samuel 5–6). One of the men of Zobah who escaped from the battle was Rezon, who then had his home in Damascus (1 Kings 11:23–4) and ruled there. Damascus grew in importance under Rezon and his successors, who became powerful adversaries of King Solomon. One of Rezon's successors was involved in conflicts between the kingdoms of Israel and Judah (2 Chronicles 16:1–4).

In the early 9th century BC the prophet Elijah was instructed by God to go to the plains of Damascus and anoint Hazael as future king of Syria (1 Kings 19:15), although he did not immediately supplant King Ben-Hadad, who continued to reign over Syria. The Israelite king Ahab overcame him in battle but spared his life when Ben-Hadad agreed to give Israel trading rights in Damascus (1 Kings 20:34). After Elijah's death, his successor, the prophet Elisha, was summoned to Damascus when King Ben-Hadad was ill. Elisha's fame as a healer had spread as a result of his curing the Damascene

Another view of the East Gate, looking down Straight Street.

commander Naaman. Hazael was sent to talk to Elisha, who told him that the king would die, as well as prophesying that Hazael as king of Syria would be a terrible enemy of Israel. Hazael hastened these events by murdering the sick king, and indeed became one of Israel's greatest scourges (2 Kings 8:7–15), although under his rule Damascus also suffered from several onslaughts by the Assyrians.

A city diminished

Under Hazael's successor Rezin the Assyrian attacks continued, until in 732 Damascus was captured by the Assyrian king Tiglath-Pileser III and its people taken captive to Kir, a city that scholars have been unable to identify (2 Kings 16:9). The city was despoiled and lost much of its wealth and political influence, as foretold by the prophet Isaiah and later evoked by Jeremiah: "Damascus is taken away from being a city, and it shall be a ruinous heap" (Isaiah 17:1); "Damascus is waxed feeble and turneth upon herself to flee" (Jeremiah 49:24). It lost its status as capital and was gradually replaced

The commercial bustle of modern city life in Straight Street.

Part of the old city wall, the same wall down which Paul escaped when officials in the city were plotting to kill him.

by Antioch as the principal city of Syria. Damascus now came under a series of different rulers and influences. The Chaldeans conquered the city in about 604 BC and the Persians around 530. After the Persian conquest the Damascene kings were allowed to reign under Persia's protection, but this ended in 333 BC when Alexander the Great captured Syria. The city was now ruled by the Seleucids, who were based at Antioch, but some western influence on Damascus came from the Greeks, who around 90 BC established a community and their own quarter in the city, remains of which can still be seen. The Romans annexed the whole region in 64 BC.

Paul in Damascus

At the time of the conversion of Saul of Tarsus, Damascus was briefly occupied by the Nabateans, an Arab merchant people who had their base in Petra. Many Jews lived in the city – perhaps a legacy from the commercial community set up by King Ahab – and a community of Christian disciples had grown up. Acts 9 describes how Saul, a devout Jew who had been a fanatical persecutor of Christians, traveled to Damascus to hunt out believers. As he came near the city he saw a great light and heard the voice of Jesus speaking to him. He was then struck blind and had to be led into Damascus, where he stayed, blind and fasting, in "the street which is called Straight."

After three days a Damascene disciple called Ananias was directed in a vision to visit Saul; Ananias laid hands upon Saul and his sight was immediately restored, after which he was baptized a Christian. Saul of Tarsus became Paul the Apostle. After his conversion he remained in Damascus for some time and began to preach his newfound faith at the synagogues, but this attracted the attention of hostile Jews and government officials who plotted to kill him. Paul had to escape over the city wall in a basket (Acts 9:25; 2 Corinthians 11:32–3) but some time later he returned to Damascus (1 Galatians 17). The reference in 2 Corinthians to the Nabatean king Aretas fixed Paul's conversion at between AD 34 and 37.

Power regained

Under Roman and then Byzantine rule Damascus began to regain some of its former importance, and trade began to flourish again. The city was fortified and many fine buildings were erected. Most of the people became Christians – but all that changed in AD 635 when Damascus was taken by the Arabs. The Byzantine cathedral was converted into a mosque. The city expanded and was converted into the capital of the Islamic Empire until 750. After that date warring dynasties ravaged the city and again its power, and most of its population, were lost.

In 1076 the Turks took Damascus and it gradually regained its former status. From that time the city alternated between Turkish and Egyptian rule. It flourished and trade increased, with Damascene goods acquiring a worldwide reputation for quality. From 1616 Damascus was capital of a Turkish province, but under 19th-century rule it once more became capital of Syria. The French occupied the city between World Wars I and II and developed it considerably, laying out the basis of the present street plan. In 1946 Damascus became capital of an independent Syria.

The tomb of Saladin, the 12th-century Muslim ruler who had his capital in Damascus and died in the city.

The tomb of St John the Baptist. The head of the Baptist is supposed to lie in a crypt in the Omayyad Mosque, though he is also traditionally believed to have been buried in the ancient town of Samaria.

The modern city has spread in all directions, particularly towards the northeast and south. Some of the old orchards have now been built over, but the surrounding fertile plains still provide the city with a plentiful supply of fruit and vegetables. In the Old City there are still traditional stone-built houses opening onto tree-lined courtyards with fountains, but new buildings are in the European style and usually of concrete.

Government bodies in Damascus superintend archeological research in Syria by local and foreign archeologists, and some exciting finds have been made of artifacts from Old Testament times. Excavation in the city itself is difficult, given its continuous occupation, but remains from various periods can still be seen in the modern city. These include the street "which is called Straight" where Paul stayed after his conversion, and parts of the city wall down which he escaped. An arcaded street and marketplace remain from the period of Greek influence and there are many remains from the 12th century Egyptian period, including the tomb of the Muslim hero Saladin, who died in the city. The 7th-century mosque, formerly the Byzantine cathedral dedicated to John the Baptist and now known as the Umayyad Mosque, has been frequently restored and still stands. The head of John the Baptist is supposedly buried in the crypt.

The Omayyad Mosque. It was originally built as a Christian cathedral in Byzantine times, but was converted to a mosque in the 7th century, and has been restored several times.

Moses in Egypt

he book of Genesis ends with Joseph and his brothers settled in Egypt. By the time of the events of the book of Exodus – probably during the 13th century BC – the number of Israelites in Egypt had increased greatly, and they were harshly oppressed and exploited by the Egyptians. At the time Moses was born this persecution had intensified to the point where the king – or Pharoah – ordered that all male Hebrew children should be killed (Exodus 1:22).

Moses' birth and upbringing

Moses was born to an Israelite woman in Egypt, who hid him for three months. Then she made a nest of bulrushes and left the baby inside it by the river bank, leaving his elder sister to watch over him. When Pharoah's daughter came there to bathe she found the child and rescued him. Moses' sister arranged for her own mother to nurse the baby until he was old enough for the princess to adopt him. Moses grew up at court, but one day he saw an Egyptian killing a Hebrew man, and retaliated by killing the Egyptian. The crime was discovered and Moses was forced to flee.

Moses and Pharoah

After many years living in the land of Midian, Moses had a vision of God, speaking to him from a burning bush. God told Moses to return to Egypt so that he could bring the oppressed Hebrews out of Egypt and lead them to a new country – a land "flowing with milk and honey." God told him he could enlist the help of his brother, Aaron, who was a more fluent spokesman.

Moses returned to Egypt, and he and Aaron spoke to the Hebrew elders, telling them of God's promise. Then they asked Pharoah to let the Israelite people go. Pharoah was not only deaf to their pleas, but he instructed the taskmasters overseeing the Hebrews to increase their labor and hardships. Moses and Aaron returned to Pharaoh many times, but he resolutely refused to release their people. After each refusal God sent a plague upon Egypt: first the rivers turned to blood, then frogs, lice, flies, boils, hailstones, locusts, and finally total darkness assailed the country. Yet still Pharaoh refused to let the Israelites leave (10:27).

This lively representation of the discovery of the infant Moses was painted by the Dutch-born British artist Sir Lawrence Alma-Tadema (1836–1912).

The Passover and the Red Sea

God's final threat to Egypt was that every firstborn in the land – both people and animals – would be killed, but still Pharoah remained unmoved. God then instructed Moses how the Hebrews could escape this fate. For a week they should eat only unleavened bread, and then take a ritual meal of lamb and bitter herbs. The lamb's blood should be used to mark their doorposts, so that the angel of death would pass over each Hebrew house without harming the inhabitants. This event is commemorated in the Jewish Passover festival.

Pharoah at last gave permission for the Israelites to leave Egypt, but after they had gone he sent horsemen and chariots to pursue them. The Israelites reached the Red Sea and God told Moses to stretch his hand over the water. A strong east wind arose and parted the sea, piling up the water on each side to make a corridor through which the Israelites could pass. The Egyptians followed, but as soon as they started crossing, God told Moses to stretch out his hand again over the sea. The water returned, drowning the Egyptians (14:28). It is believed that the crossing of the Red Sea took place at the region of the Bitter Lakes, just north of Suez, where the water is shallow and full of reeds and to this day can be driven back by a strong east wind.

This famous statue of the Ephesian form of Artemis depicts her with many breasts, which gives rise to speculation that the Greek goddess took over a cult attached to an existing fertility goddess in Ephesus.

An arch from the temple of Hadrian, dating from the 1st century AD.

EPHESUS

Famed in ancient times for its immense temple of Artemis, Ephesus was the scene of St Paul's stormiest confrontation with the pagans.

The city of Ephesus was capital of the Roman province of Asia. It stood at the mouth of a branch of the River Cayster in what is now western Turkey. This once magnificent city has lain in ruins for centuries, but has been extensively studied by archeologists for many years.

The city of Artemis

It is best known in Biblical terms for its association with the Apostle Paul (Acts 18:19–19:41, 20:17; 1 Corinthians 15:32, 16:8–9; Ephesians). There was probably a settlement of some kind at Ephesus from the 12th century BC, but the city was established in the 10th century when Ionian colonists joined the Anatolian settlers and built on the site. Silt washed down the river made the land rich and fertile, but also gradually blocked up the harbor, so that the ruins of the city are now about 6 miles (10 km) inland.

It is not clear when the cult of Artemis was first established at Ephesus. It is probable that worship of the Greek huntress goddess was preceded by the cult of a more ancient mother or fertility goddess, for the famous statue that stood in the temple was adorned with many breasts. The huge and magnificent temple of Artemis, one of the Seven Wonders of the World, was built about 550 BC by Croesus, the Lydian king who ruled over the city, on the site of an existing temple to the goddess.

Croesus was defeated in 546 by Cyrus and Ephesus fell under Persian rule, but subsequently became subject to Athens and then to Sparta. Around 286 BC it was conquered by the Macedonian general Lysimachus. Under Croesus the city was centered around the temple of Artemis, but Lysimachus based his administration in the harbor area.

The city began to prosper and its population grew rapidly. It briefly became part of the kingdom of Pergamum, but was then handed over to the Romans in 133 BC.

New Testament Ephesus

Ephesus flourished and grew under Roman rule. The temple of Artemis, rebuilt after a fire in 356 BC, was still the focus of the city's religious life. There were also three temples devoted to the cult of the emperor, and many other impressive public buildings, including a huge theater and a triumphal arch.

Like many major cities in the Roman empire, Ephesus had acquired a large Jewish population, who were apparently respected and

This capital is typical of the architecture found in the Roman ruins of Ephesus.

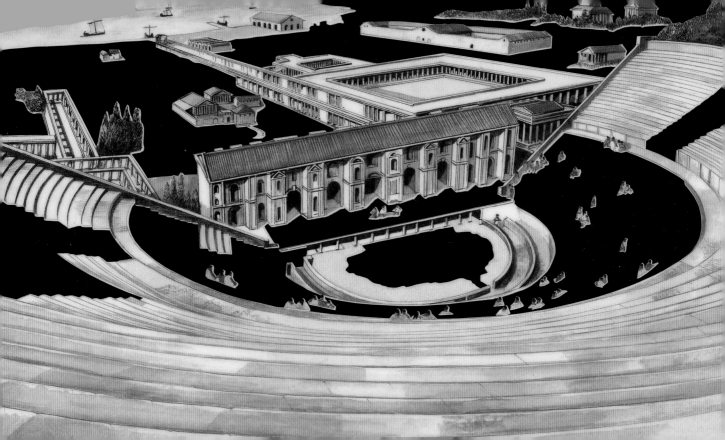

The reconstruction shows the classical Greek city, with the great theater in the foreground. The sea cannot be seen on the modern picture, for it has moved several miles westwards.

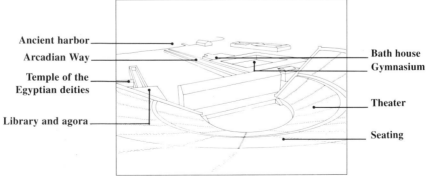

Ancient harbor

Arcadian Way

Temple of the
Egyptian deities

Library and agora

Bath house

Gymnasium

Theater

Seating

THE RIOT IN EPHESUS

Paul made a brief trip to Ephesus in the course of his second missionary journey (Acts 18:18–21), but during his third journey he spent two years in the city.

Acts 19 describes how Paul came to Ephesus for the second time and found disciples there who had only a sketchy knowledge of Christianity. He instructed them further and baptized them, and they received the Holy Spirit. Paul then embarked on a campaign of preaching.

An illustration of Acts 18:19 showing the Ephesians burning their precious books of magic arts. The central figure is presumably Paul.

Paul's teaching began to have profound effects on the culture of the city. Some Jews who had been involved in exorcism and various magical cults renounced their former practices, burned their books of magic, and accepted the Christian gospel. But the most significant effect was on the cult of Diana, the goddess of the city. There was a flourishing industry in Ephesus manufacturing statuettes of Diana and other artifacts relating to the worship of the goddess. Now Paul was declaring that the true God cannot be worshiped through manufactured statues and temples, and drawing many away from the cult of Diana.

A silversmith called Demetrius, who made his living through crafting shrines for Diana, called a meeting of artisans whose trade was suffering because of the new religion. He reminded them that Paul had brought about a revolution in the city and throughout the province, not only damaging their trade, but bringing the great goddess and her worship into disrepute. He whipped his audience up into a fury of indignation, and they started to chant "Great is Diana of the Ephesians." A riot ensued: the crowd stormed the theater and captured two of Paul's Macedonian companions.

Eventually the riot was quelled by the town clerk, the chief city official responsible to the Romans. He told them that the town's reputation for worship of

One of a series of statues from Ephesus symbolizing wisdom, knowledge, virtue, and intelligence, all attributes valued highly in classical culture.

Diana was so strong that it could not be seriously damaged, that the men that they were accusing were apparently innocent, and that if Demetrius and his fellow artisans had any charge to bring against them they could do it through the proper lawful channels. As soon as the uproar had died down, Paul left Ephesus for Greece.

well treated under Roman rule. However, it seems that the new religion of Christianity had made little impact on the city at the time that Paul first visited it around AD 52. It was not until Paul's longer stay in the city a few years later that the Christian faith began to win large numbers of adherents, from both the Jewish and the Gentile populations. The cult of Diana (as Artemis was known to the Romans) clearly suffered, and a church was established in the city. This church was the recipient of one of Paul's letters, and was the first of the seven churches of Asia to be addressed by John in the book of Revelation (2:1–7).

The city declines

In AD 262 Ephesus was invaded by Goths, who wrecked much of the city and completely destroyed the temple of Artemis, which was never rebuilt. After this the city never recovered its former prominence, although it was still important enough in the eastern Church for the Third General Council to be held there in 431. A new cult arose shortly after: that of the "Seven Sleepers," martyrs of the 3rd century who were supposedly raised from the dead.

Constant silting gradually separated Ephesus from the sea, making the port useless, and over the years it declined into a small town, which probably lost its population at some time during the late Middle Ages.

A British archeologist excavated the theater and the 2nd century AD odeum (concert hall) between 1863 and 1874, and finally discovered part of the ruined temple of Artemis. Further excavations throughout the 20th century have revealed more of the temple – both Croesus' original and the later rebuilding – and the remains of many other public buildings.

Though much of the older Hellenistic Ephesus remains hidden, it is now possible to gain a clear idea of the layout of the Roman town. The streets were as usual laid out in a rectangular pattern, and buildings include the great theater, the rather smaller odeum, the agora, library, and gymnasiums, as well as fountains, aqueducts, and baths. There are also the remains of several churches, including the basilica dedicated to the Virgin Mary and the church of the Seven Sleepers.

Above left: *Remains of the 2nd-century AD odeum, discovered in the 19th century.*
Above: *The library of Celsus, built during the reign of the Roman emperor Trajan in the 2nd century AD.*

Above: *The Roman Arcadian Way, which leads to the theater.*
Right: *A view of the Roman Curetes Street, which leads to the agora.*

NINEVEH

Nineveh, the oldest city of Assyria and its last capital, is celebrated in the Bible for the wickedness of its inhabitants and prophesies of its destruction.

This ancient bronze head which is thought to represent King Sargon I was found in the ruins of Nineveh.

Nineveh stood on the east bank of the Tigris, across the river from what is now Mosul in northern Iraq. It features in the Old Testament in the story of Jonah, the accounts of Sennacherib's attacks on Judah, and various prophecies of the city's ultimate doom.

Nineveh in prehistory

Like Babylon, Nineveh was said to have been founded by the great hunter Nimrod (Genesis 10:11). In fact the site was first settled in Neolithic times, probably as early as the 7th millennium BC. Excavations have revealed evidence of life and economic activity in prehistoric Nineveh, including pottery, metalwork, and beads. Many of these artifacts show the influence of southern Mesopotamia, suggesting that before 3000 BC the towns of the Tigris and the Euphrates were connected by trading interests. The most impressive find from this period is a life-size bronze head of a monarch, probably dating from about 2250 BC, and possibly representing King Sargon or King Naram-Sin, both of whom have been suggested as the ruler on whom the Biblical Nimrod was based.

It was not until about 1250 BC that Nineveh began to gain importance, although there was some building before that date. The son of Sargon built a temple to the goddess Ishtar in about 2300 BC; and inscriptions describe how this was restored in 1800, improved by Hammurapi of Babylon, and then restored again in 1230 BC. The Hebrew name Nineveh derives ultimately from a Sumerian form of the name of Ishtar, the goddess who was worshiped throughout Assyria. Nineveh began to be used as a royal residence; palaces and temples were built by Tiglath Pileser I, Ashurnasirpal II, and Sargon II.

The events of the book of Jonah, which describe the people of Nineveh repenting of their wicked ways, probably relate to the period before the accession of Tiglath Pileser I, although the book was apparently written after the fall of Nineveh. It describes Jonah taking three days to walk through the city (3:4), which suggests that a larger area than the city itself was in question, for a city with a surrounding wall only 7½ miles (12 km) long could not have taken so long to walk through. God speaks of it to Jonah as having 120,000 inhabitants (4:11), which tallies well with the size of the city as revealed by excavations.

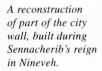

*A reconstruction
of part of the city
wall, built during
Sennacherib's reign
in Nineveh.*

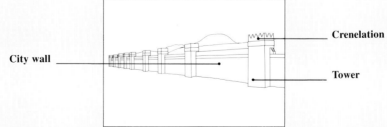

City wall

Crenelation

Tower

Sennacherib and his successors

Sennacherib, who ruled Assyria from 705 to 681 BC, was responsible for transforming Nineveh into a great city. He made it his capital, building an aqueduct that provided a fresh water supply for the city and irrigated the parks, laying out new streets and squares, and erecting new buildings. The most impressive of these was what he called a "palace without a rival," a huge 80-room building decorated with sculpture and relief carvings, many of which depicted his victories. He rebuilt the fortifications, constructing massive brick walls with 15 large and elaborately decorated gateways built of brick and stone. Archeological research has enabled a reconstruction of several of these great gates. The Nergal Gate was flanked by two stone figures of winged bulls, and the Shamash Gate was surrounded by two moats and fortified with six towers.

Sennacherib's assault on Judah and the tribute he forced from King Hezekiah are described in 2 Kings 18:13–16. Sennacherib

A marble slab from Nineveh 705–681 BC depicts Sennacherib building his palace, and features a gigantic bull.

himself, writing of the campaign, says that he shut up "Hezekiah the Jew . . . like a caged bird within his royal capital, Jerusalem." In 2 Kings 19 and Isaiah 36 and 37 we are told how Hezekiah consulted the prophet Isaiah, who prophesied the defeat of Sennacherib. After the rout of his army Sennacherib returned to Nineveh, where shortly afterwards

A reconstruction of the Shamash Gate, one of the 15 great gates built during Sennacherib's reign, 705–681 BC.

JONAH IN NINEVEH

The Old Testament book of Jonah centers around the prophet's mission to preach repentance to the city of Nineveh, renowned for the wickedness of its people.

In the first chapter Jonah hears the Lord speaking to him, saying: "Arise, go to Nineveh, that great city, and cry against it; for their wickedness is come up before me." Clearly this was a daunting task, which Jonah did not feel equal to. Instead of making his way to Nineveh, he went to the port of Joppa, where he found a ship bound for Tarshish. (The identity of Tarshish has not been established, although many scholars believe it to have been Tartessus in Spain.)

But God raised a wind and brought about a violent tempest. The terrified sailors began to pray to their various gods for deliverance. Jonah had slept through all this tumult, but the ship's captain woke him, telling him to pray to his god. Now the sailors began to surmise that one of their number had caused this disaster to come upon them, so they cast lots to see who it was; the lot fell upon Jonah.

The sailors questioned Jonah, who told them that he was a Hebrew and a believer in the Lord who had created earth and sea, but that he was fleeing from the Lord's presence. He told them that it was because of his disobedience that God had caused the tempest and that if they threw him overboard, the sea would become calm. Although the sailors were reluctant to do this, when the storm continued to rage they decided that there was no alternative so they threw Jonah into the sea, which immediately became calm. The awestruck sailors made vows of allegiance to God. Jonah himself was swallowed by "a great fish," in whose belly he remained for three days and three nights, after which the fish vomited him up onto the land.

The final two chapters describe how Jonah heard the voice of the Lord once more commanding him to go to Nineveh, and how this time he obeyed. As the Lord had instructed him, he warned the people that because of their wickedness their city would be destroyed in 40 days. His message was heeded: all the people of Nineveh, from the king to the lowliest inhabitant, repented, fasting and covering themselves in sackcloth and ashes, and crying to God for mercy. God, seeing their repentance, decided that he would be merciful and would not destroy the city.

Jonah became very angry that the Lord had made him prophesy destruction to Nineveh, and had then failed to carry out this threat, and he actually reproached God for his merciful nature, asking God to kill him, for his life was now not worth living. He went to the eastern side of the city and made himself a shelter there. God caused a large gourd to grow up, to provide shade to protect Jonah from the heat, but the next morning he caused a worm to attack the gourd, which withered and died. When the sun rose Jonah was faint from the heat and again he wished for death, but God told him that just as Jonah felt sorry for the loss of the gourd, so God would have felt sorry for the loss of the people of Nineveh, on whom he had taken pity because they were not capable of knowing right from wrong.

This 16th-century engraving depicts various aspects of the Jonah story: in the center he is shown being cast from the ship and swallowed by the fish; in the foreground he is spewed out of the fish's mouth; on the right of the picture he is sitting under the gourd in Nineveh.

he was assassinated by his own sons while worshiping in the temple of Nisroch.

Sennacherib was succeeded by Esarhaddon, who continued to build in Nineveh. His son Ashurbanipal, who reigned from 669 to 627 BC, built a new palace and a fine library, for which he collected scholarly texts from all over Mesopotamia. These included scientific, literary, and religious texts, and political and administrative documents.

The fall of Nineveh

In 612 BC a combined force of Babylonians, Medes, and Scythians attacked Nineveh and sacked the city, burning most of it to the ground. The king, Sinsharishkin, died in the fire, and all the great buildings fell. Nineveh was never to recover from this devastation. Its fall had been predicted by the prophet Nahum. The three chapters of the book of Nahum are devoted to prophesying the destruction of the city. The prophet Zephaniah also predicted that God "will make Nineveh a desolation, and dry like a wilderness" (2:13). Although Nineveh was almost entirely ruined in 612, and was never to be rebuilt as a city again, it was intermittently inhabited at various times, and there is evidence that there were still people living there as late as the 16th century AD.

Archeological finds at Nineveh

Travelers who saw the ruins of the city in the 17th and 18th centuries thought it

Another reconstruction of the huge brick walls and decorative gates that Sennacherib built to fortify the city.

A relief from the North Palace of about 650 BC shows defeated Elamites being led away by Assyrians after Ashurbanipal had sacked their city.

likely that they had discovered the site of the Biblical Nineveh. However, it was not until the mid-19th century that its identity was firmly established. The pioneering work can be credited to the English explorer, archeologist, and Member of Parliament Sir Austen Henry Layard. In 1845 he began an excavation of the ruins of Nimrud, south of Mosul, and now known to be the site of Calah (Genesis 10:11), which was destroyed at the same time as Nineveh. Believing this to be the site of Nineveh, Layard began excavations and found many treasures here from the reign of King Ashurbanipal.

Turning to the ruins opposite Mosul, Layard at last discovered the real site of Nineveh, unearthing the palace of Sennacherib and many cuneiform tablets from the great library which provided invaluable and fascinating information on the life and culture of Assyria and Babylon. All Layard's finds were taken to the British Museum and can still be seen there. Later in the 19th century studies of the discoveries from the library of Ashburnipal identified some of the tablets as the great Babylonian *Epic of Gilgamesh*, which describes the great flood in similar terms to those of Genesis 7.

Many of Layard's findings related to episodes described in the Bible. A black marble obelisk shows Jehu, king of Israel, paying tribute to the Assyrian king Shalmanezer. Carved reliefs from the palace clearly depict the Assyrian capture of Lachish (2 Kings 18:14) by Sennacherib.

Later excavations, mainly sponsored by the British Museum, continued into the 20th century. In the 1960s the work was taken over by the Iraqi government, who have restored much of Sennacherib's palace and the great gates of the city. Iraqi archeologists have also unearthed previously undiscovered treasures from the palace, including many carved upright stone slabs illustrated with representations of Sennacherib's military campaigns. Most of the carvings and inscriptions relating to the Assyrian battles with Israel and Judah, and their exaction of tribute, correspond fairly well with the scriptural accounts, although it seems likely that the Assyrian accounts exaggerate their victories and underestimate their defeats, while the Bible does the opposite.

Above: *A detail from the black marble obelisk found by Layard at Nineveh. It shows King Jehu bowing to the Assyrian king Shalmanezer III.*

Below: *A relief from Sennacherib's palace, dating from 702 BC and showing a Phoenician warship.*

THE PERSIAN EMPIRE

The Persian Empire took over from the Babylonian Empire as the dominant force in western Asia in the 6th and 5th centuries BC. The Persians enjoyed an advanced culture and enormous wealth. Gold ornaments and jewelry have been found in the ruins of ancient palaces, including the winter palace at Susa. Many Jews who had been taken into captivity in Babylon remained in the Persian Empire.

King Ahasuerus

King Ahasuerus reigned over Persia from 485 to 465 BC. The first chapter of Esther describes how the king gave a great feast for all the men in Susa, while his wife Vashti entertained the women. After the feast had been going on for a week, the king summoned his wife so that he could show off her beauty to his guests, but Vashti refused to be displayed. Ahasuerus was angry and asked his wise men for advice. They declared that the king must divorce Vashti, for if he appeared to condone her disobedience it would set a bad example to all the wives in Persia. Ahasuerus followed their counsel, and his advisers then suggested that he send messengers to seek out all the beautiful young virgins in the land, from whose number he could choose a new wife.

Esther and Mordecai

There was a Jew called Mordecai living in Susa with his orphaned cousin Esther, whom he had brought up as his own daughter. When his beautiful protégée was chosen to be taken to the royal harem, Mordecai advised her to keep her Jewish race a secret. The young women selected were given a year's beauty treatment before being presented one by one to the king; some spent just one night with him while others who took his fancy might go to him again if he asked for them. When Esther was brought before Ahasuerus he liked her more than any of the others, and decided to marry her. She was crowned queen and Mordecai was given an administrative post at the palace.

Haman's plot

Ahasuerus promoted a man called Haman as prime minister and decreed that all his officials show respect to the new premier by kneeling to him.

All obeyed except Mordecai, and when his colleagues asked him the reason for his refusal he admitted that he was a Jew. They reported this to Haman, who was so furious that he vowed not only to punish Mordecai but to kill all the Jews in the empire. He told Ahasuerus that he should no longer tolerate these rebellious people in his kingdom, and got the king's permission to issue a proclamation that all Jews in the empire were to be killed.

A portrayal of Queen Esther and her cousin Mordecai, by the 15th-century Italian artist Andrea Mantegna.

When Mordecai heard of this he began to mourn, putting on sackcloth and ashes. He sent Esther a message explaining what Haman had done and warning her not to reveal her race, lest she too should die. Esther replied to Mordecai with a message to gather all the Jews in Susa together and to fast and pray for three days. She then invited the king and Haman to a banquet, where she pleased the king so much he offered her anything she wanted. She merely asked them to feast with her again the next evening. Meanwhile, Haman erected a gallows on which to hang Morecai.

That night the king discovered that Mordecai had once foiled a plot to assassinate him, but had never been rewarded. When Haman appeared, ready to ask for Mordecai to be hanged, the king told him that there was someone he wished to honor. Haman, assuming he was the person in question, advised the king to give the man new robes and public acknowledgment, and then had to endure seeing Mordecai honored as he himself had suggested.

At Esther's banquet that night the king again asked her what she wanted for herself, and at last she told the king that all her race were to be destroyed because of Haman's wickedness. Haman was hanged on the gallows he had built for Mordecai, but it was not possible to revoke the royal proclamation. However, the king allowed Mordecai to send out letters to all the Jews in the empire warning them to defend themselves. Armed and ready, the Jews defeated their enemies. These events are still celebrated every year in the Jewish festival of Purim.

CYPRUS

*The legendary birthplace of the goddess Aphrodite, Cyprus was
also the birthplace of the Apostle Barnabas, and the island was
one of the first places in Europe to accept Christianity.*

A large island in the Eastern
Mediterranean, Cyprus lies at equal
distance from the coasts of Syria and
Turkey. It has been inhabited since Late
Neolithic times, and fought over bitterly
because of its mineral wealth.

The island of copper

The island features in the New Testament
Book of Acts (4:36, 13:4–12, 15:39, 27:4). It
is also thought to appear in the Old Testament
under different names, although many
modern translations actually use the name
Cyprus. It is called Chittim in Numbers
24:24; Isaiah 23:1, 12; Jeremiah 2:10; Ezekiel
27:6; it is Elisha in Ezzekiel 27:7.

Early settlements in Cyprus have left traces
of beehive houses and stone utensils of the
Late Neolithic period, dating back to the
middle of the 6th millennium BC. The early
3rd millennium saw the first use of copper,
the metal for which the island became
famous. Our word "copper" is derived from
the Latin name cyprium, "from Cyprus."

The Middle Bronze Age culture of Cyprus
shows influences from Asia Minor and Syria,
but by the Late Bronze Age the main
influence came from the Minoan civilization
of Crete. By the 14th century BC Mycenean
traders had begun to settle on Cyprus,
followed by Achean colonizers who
brought Greek culture and language,
established a tradition of kingship,
and developed the copper-mining
industry. It was probably copper
that gained the island its fame, for

*The remains of a
sanctuary sacred to
Apollo, one of the most
widely worshiped of the
Greek gods.*

Above: *A 14th-century
BC Mycenean crater – a
jar used for mixing
wine and water – found
at Enkomi. It shows a
chariot and Zeus
holding the scales
of destiny.*

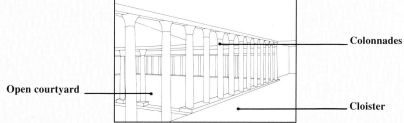

A reconstruction of the ancient gymnasium at Salamis on the east coast of Cyprus. Once the island's principal city, Salamis was largely destroyed in the 7th century AD.

Open courtyard

Colonnades

Cloister

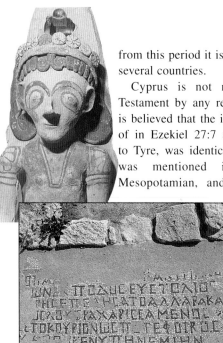

from this period it is named in the records of several countries.

Cyprus is not mentioned in the Old Testament by any recognizable name, but it is believed that the island of Elishah, spoken of in Ezekiel 27:7 as exporting purple dye to Tyre, was identical with Alashiya, which was mentioned in various Egyptian, Mesopotamian, and other sources as an exporter of copper. The name Alashiya is thought to refer to Enkomi on the east coast, where excavations have revealed evidence of a busy trading post in the Late Bronze Age. There is also an association between Cyprus and Kittim (or Chittim), a name applied variously in the Old Testament to a seafaring people and the place they came from (Numbers 24:24; Isaiah 23:1, 12; Ezekiel 27:6). Elishah and Kittim were originally the names of two of the sons of Javan among whom the "isles of the Gentiles" were divided (Genesis 10:4–5). The settlement of Kittim may well have developed into the city of Kition, near modern Larnaka. Both "Elishah" and "Kittim" were used to refer to the whole island of Cyprus, as well as to the specific cities.

By the 9th century BC trade was well established between Cyprus and Syria, Palestine, and Egypt, as well as with Rhodes and mainland Greece. Around the year 800 Phoenician settlers began to infiltrate the island, settling particularly in Kition. Many inscriptions from this period have been found.

In 709 BC the Cypriot kings began to pay tribute to the Assyrian king Sargon II.

Top: *This terracotta statuette of a woman worshiper demonstrates Cypriot workmanship of the 7th century BC.*
Above: *An inscription from the ancient city of Curium.*

However, Assyrian dominance lasted for only about 40 years, after which Cyprus enjoyed nearly 100 years of independence. During this century fine palaces were built for the increasingly powerful kings, shipbuilding and copper mining thrived, and culture flourished, particularly in ceramics and silverware.

In 560 BC the island was captured by the Egyptians. Their rule was soon superseded by that of the Persians, who dominated the island until it was conquered by Alexander the Great in 333 BC. This new rule, too, was brief and Cyprus soon came under the rule of the Ptolemies of Egypt, during which period Jews first began to settle on the island.

Roman and Byzantine Cyprus

In 58 BC Cyprus was annexed by the Romans and a few years later was incorporated into Cilicia. In 27 BC it became a province of the Roman Empire, and by New Testament times

A mosaic from Curium, representing Creation.

Below: *St Barnabas Monastery in Salamis. Paul's friend and companion, Barnabas was born and probably died on Cyprus.*

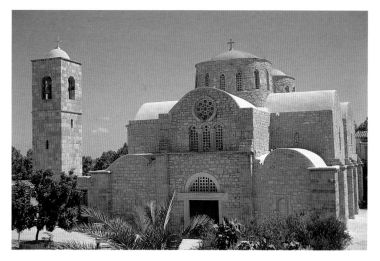

PAUL AND BARNABAS IN CYPRUS

When Paul and Barnabas were sent out from the church at Antioch as missionaries to the Gentile world, Cyprus was their first destination. The story of their visit is told in Acts 13:4–12. Accompanied by John Mark, a cousin of Barnabas, they landed at Salamis, where they preached in the synagogues, and then traveled across the island to Paphos.

In Paphos they were summoned by the Roman governor of the island, the proconsul Sergius Paulus, an intelligent man who had presumably heard reports of their preaching and wanted to hear it for himself. However, Sergius Paulus had a friend called Bar-Jesus (or Elymas in Greek), a Jewish sorcerer who claimed to be a prophet. When Paul and Barnabas attempted to preach the gospel to Sergius Paulus, Bar-Jesus did all he could to obstruct them and prevent his friend from hearing and accepting the faith.

Then Paul, filled with the Holy Spirit, looked the magician straight in the eyes and said, "O full of all subtilty and all mischief, thou child of the devil, thou enemy of all righteousness, wilt thou not cease to pervert the right ways of the Lord? And now, behold, the hand of the Lord is upon thee, and thou shalt be blind, not seeing the sun for a season."

Immediately the eyes of Bar-Jesus were covered by a dark mist, and he was unable to find his way without someone to lead him by the hand. Sergius Paulus was amazed by this manifestation of the power of the Lord, and accepted the message that Paul and Barnabas preached to him.

An engraving of St Barnabas, who preached in Cyprus as early as AD 45 or 46.

S. BARNABAS APOSTOLUS.

it was governed by a proconsul. The island is first mentioned in the New Testament as the home of Barnabas, a disciple in the Jerusalem church who was to become the friend and companion of the Apostle Paul (Acts 4:36). Although he later became subsidiary in importance to Paul, originally Barnabas was the senior member of the partnership and Paul was his protégé. There were several Cypriots among the earliest converts to Christianity, and the island became a refuge for Christians fleeing persecution in Jerusalem. Cypriots helped to establish the church at Antioch, being the first to preach to the Greek Gentiles there (Acts 11:19–20).

Paul and Barnabas visited Cyprus at the start of their first missionary journey, and based their activities in Paphos. This was "New Paphos," a Roman foundation on the coast that had become the center of Roman rule on the island. "Old Paphos," now Kouklia, was a much older Phoenician town slightly inland, famed for its shrine to the goddess Aphrodite. Barnabas returned to Cyprus with his cousin John Mark, after his disagreement with Paul over this disciple

Above: *The Rock of Aphrodite on the Cypriot coast. The goddess is reputed to have been born from the sea foam near Paphos.* **Left:** *The remains of a Roman gymnasium at Salamis.*

caused them to part company (Acts 15:36–39). After this, Cyprus is mentioned only in passing in the book of Acts, but the church there continued to grow, as evidenced by the fact that it sent a delegation of three bishops to the Council of Nicea in AD 325.

In AD 115 the Jews of Cyprus revolted against Roman rule, killing thousands and largely destroying the city of Salamis. The Emperor Hadrian subsequently expelled all Jews from the island. Roman rule lasted until 395, and extensive archeological remains from this period have been found, including tombs, glassware, and sculpture.

For 700 years Cyprus was subject to the Byzantine emperors. The church was at first governed from Antioch, but it established its independence in 431 and has remained to this day an autonomous church within the Orthodox community. For about 300 years from the mid-7th century Cyprus was subject to constant Muslim raids, with the Byzantine emperors of Constantinople and their Islamic enemies using the island as a convenient base from which to launch attacks on each other.

In 1191 Richard I of England conquered the island and then sold it to Guy de Lusignan, the dispossessed Crusader King of Jerusalem, who established a feudal monarchy with an aristocracy whose language and culture were French and entirely divorced from those of the native population. Trade, however, was largely with Italy, and Italian influence increased until the 15th century, when Cyprus became part of the Venetian Empire. In 1570 Cyprus was taken by the Ottoman Turks, who ruled it for 300 years. There were

The remains of the Temple of Apollo, the sun god, who was associated with prophecy, healing, music and poetry.

several revolts and agitation for self-government, but the reform movement achieved little. In 1878 the British took over the administration of Cyprus, although the Turks still kept their sovereignty. The British annexed the island at the outbreak of war with Turkey in 1914.

Union and division

In 1924 Cyprus became a British crown colony, but from the beginning there was violent conflict, with demands from the Greek majority for Enosis, union with Greece – a movement fiercely resisted by the Turkish minority. During the 1950s the conflict escalated and British troops were sent to Cyprus. In 1960 the island became an independent republic, with a government that included both Greek and Turkish Cypriots, and the following year it became part of the British Commonwealth. But the new power-sharing constitution was unworkable and the strife continued.

The leader of the Enosis movement had been the Orthodox patriarch Archbishop Makarios, who became president of the new republic, sparking off an ecclesiastical controversy about the conflict between his spiritual and political roles. He was deposed in a coup in 1974, which led to Turkish troops invading Cyprus and occupying one-third of the island. The occupied area then became the self-styled Turkish Republic of Northern Cyprus, recognized only by Turkey.

The country is still largely rural and agricultural, but there has been some drift to the cities. The Greek majority, who make up about four-fifths of the population, are mainly Eastern Orthodox Christians, while the Turkish minority are almost all Muslims.

Archeological discoveries

Most of the archeological research in Cyprus has been carried out in the 20th century, since the British occupation. Investigations have been organized by British, American, French, and Swedish archeologists, as well as by local Cypriot scholars.

The earliest finds come from the settlements of the 6th millennium BC, when stone and flint utensils were used. There have been significant finds from slightly later periods, and there is evidence of how the original beehive dwellings were replaced by more sophisticated circular houses, and how the combed ceramics of the 4th century developed into the island's characteristic painted pottery.

Cypriot pottery developed to become, along with copper, one of the island's most exportable commodities, although the actual pots were often merely the most convenient method of transporting the contents, which may have been oil or opium. The distinctive red and black painted pots of the Late Bronze Age, often decorated with pictures of birds and fishes, have been found not only in Cyprus but throughout the whole of Palestine, and in Egypt and Syria.

Many of the discoveries date from the period of Phoenician settlement. As well as many funerary and other inscriptions, Phoenician-influenced objects such as gold jewelry and silver and bronze bowls have been found, mainly on the site of Kition outside Larnaka, where a Phoenician temple was excavated in the early 1970s. It was probably built on the site of earlier temples, and is rectangular with a colonnade. Interestingly, this find has provided evidence against the theory that Solomon's Temple in Jerusalem was of Phoenician design, for the Kition building shows no similarities to the Temple.

Other important excavations have been undertaken at Kouklia (Old Paphos), where articles from the 5th century BC showing Egyptian and Persian influence have been found; and at Enkomi, where Late Bronze Age pottery and metal artifacts were discovered. Considerable evidence of the Roman period has been found at Paphos, and also at the ancient site of Salamis, a town on the east coast near modern Famagusta, which was second in importance only to Paphos and eventually became the island's most important trading center until it was destroyed by a series of earthquakes. Roman remains on these sites include copper coins, bronze and marble statuary, and glassware.

Above and left: The Tomb of the Kings is one of the most impressive remains found at Old Paphos, or Kouklia, the old Phoenician town devoted to the cult of the goddess Aphrodite.

The chapel in the catacombs from the Roman period at Paphos.

Mountains of the Old Testament

The Hebrew words used to describe hilly places are rather unspecific. What is translated as "mountain" might be what we would call a mountain, it might be a whole mountain range or a hilly tract of land, or it might be what we would define as no more than a hill. Together with the fact that place-names change over the years, this often makes it difficult to identify a particular "mountain" referred to in the Scriptures.

Mount Carmel

Mount Carmel is the highest peak of a range of mountains in northwest Israel. It is mentioned often in the Old Testament, but the most famous story associated with it concerns the prophet Elijah at the time when Ahab and Jezebel reigned (1 Kings 18). Elijah took on the prophets of the god Baal by arranging a contest on Mount Carmel to see whose god could produce fire to burn an offering; the prophets of Baal failed utterly, while Elijah's God miraculously answered him with fire. The Carmelite Order originated with a monastery near the site in 1155.

This 16th-century Turkish painting shows the angel bringing a ram for Abraham to sacrifice in place of his son.

Mount Sinai

Mount Sinai is best known as the mountain where God appeared to Moses and handed down the Ten Commandments (Exodus 19–20). However, though the mountain in question is clearly located in the Sinai Peninsula, its identity is not obvious and three different mountains have been thought by scholars to be the Biblical Mount Sinai. The best contender is Jabal Mūsā, which rises to 7,490 feet (2,285 m), and has traditionally been regarded as Mount Sinai for over 1,500 years. A monastery, built in AD 530, stands at the foot of the mountain.

Jabal Mūsā, situated in the wilderness region of the Sinai Peninsula.

An illuminated letter from the medieval Winchester Bible showing the story of Elijah on Mount Carmel.

Mount Moriah

Genesis 22 tells the story of how Abraham obeyed God by taking his son Isaac to a mountain in "the land of Moriah" and preparing to sacrifice him there. Moriah is otherwise mentioned in the Bible only in 2 Chronicles 3:1, as the place where Solomon built the temple. Because of this reference, and because the distance from the Philistine country where Abraham was living and Jerusalem might well have required the three-day journey mentioned, Mount Moriah has traditionally been assumed to be the hill where the temple was built. Temple Mount now of course is the site of the Dome of the Rock mosque.

JERICHO

Jericho is famed as the city miraculously conquered by Joshua, and also features in many Gospel stories.

Above: *A jar in the shape of a deer's head, dating from the 2nd millennium BC.*
Right: *A circular tower from the Neolithic period (8000–7000 BC) of the Jericho city wall.* **Below:** *Tell-el-Sultan, the site of the Neolithic city, showing trenches dug in Kenyon's excavations.*

The name Jericho (Ariha in Arabic) probably derives from the name of a Semitic moon god. This ancient city, west of the River Jordan and 5 miles (8 km) north of the Dead Sea, has been frequently destroyed and rebuilt and has changed its site at least three times. The modern Jordanian town stands among the ruins of a score of successive cities. Despite its site in the desert, 820 feet (250 m) below sea level, a natural freshwater spring creates an oasis of fertile land that has attracted settlers there for thousands of years.

An ancient civilization

Jericho is one of the oldest continuously settled areas in the world. There is evidence that hunters of the Mesolithic period began to set up huts there in about 9000 BC. By 8000 BC an agricultural settlement had developed and a stone wall had been built around it. For the next two thousand years a Neolithic culture grew up, with housing becoming more sophisticated and the development of agriculture based on irrigation. One of the archeological finds from the Neolithic period is a section of stone wall with the remains of

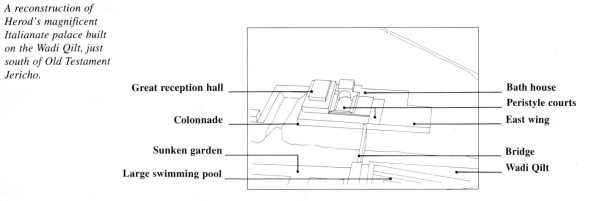

A reconstruction of Herod's magnificent Italianate palace built on the Wadi Qilt, just south of Old Testament Jericho.

Great reception hall

Colonnade

Sunken garden

Large swimming pool

Bath house

Peristyle courts

East wing

Bridge

Wadi Qilt

. . . AND THE WALLS CAME TUMBLING DOWN

The story of how Joshua and his army captured the city of Jericho is told in Joshua 6. The Israelites had entered Canaan and were camped by the banks of the Jordan, planning how to take Jericho. The city was closed for fear of an Israelite attack, with the walls guarded and the gates locked, and nobody went in or out.

God spoke to Joshua, giving him precise instructions. The onslaught on Jericho was to involve the priests as well as the army. An advance guard of soldiers was to go before a group of seven priests bearing trumpets of rams' horns; behind these the Ark of the Covenant would be carried, followed by a rearguard. Joshua assembled the troops and priests in this manner, and early in the morning the procession marched once around the walls of Jericho. The priests blew on their trumpets, but Joshua had told the people that they must not shout or make any sound until he gave them leave. The second day they did exactly the same thing, and so on for six days.

On the seventh day the procession marched around the city not once but seven times. And on the seventh circuit, when the priests blew on their trumpets Joshua commanded all the people to shout. The trumpets blew, the people all shouted loudly, and the walls of Jericho fell down.

The Israelites then entered the city and, on Joshua's instructions, they killed every living thing in it and destroyed with fire all goods except the silver, gold, and iron vessels, which were kept for the Lord's treasury. The only inhabitants of Jericho who escaped with their lives were the household of Rahab, a prostitute who had previously given shelter to the men Joshua had sent to spy out the land (Joshua 2:1–21).

A rather unpleasant postscript to the story follows in the story of Achan (Joshua 7). Achan was one of those who was involved in the attack on Jericho, but he disobeyed Joshua's order to destroy all the spoils that they found in the city apart from the metal vessels reserved for the Lord's treasury. Achan was tempted by "a goodly Babylonish garment" as well as some silver and gold that he found; he took them and hid them under his tent. Joshua discovered this violation when his army failed to take the city of Ai, and God told him that this was because there was "an accursed thing" among them. Achan confessed his theft, and he and all his family were stoned to death.

An illustration of the story from Joshua 6, showing the priests with their rams' horns preceding those carrying the Ark of the Covenant.

Right: *A vase in the shape of a human head, dating from about 15th century BC Jericho.*
Far right: *Elisha's fountain, traditional site of the spring that the prophet made wholesome when he was living in Jericho (2 Kings 2:19–22).*

a circular tower with interior steps. Another fascinating discovery from this period is a set of plaster heads molded around human skulls and possibly associated with a cult of ancestor worship. After about 6000 BC Jericho was only intermittently inhabited; remains from this period include pottery.

From about 3200 BC Jericho became a settled walled city once more but in about 2300 it was invaded by a nomadic people, probably Amorites, and then around 1900 – in the Middle Bronze Age – it was settled by the Canaanites. During the Biblical period of the patriarchs Abraham, Isaac, and Jacob, the city was home to a fairly advanced civilization. Much of our knowledge of Jericho in this period comes from the discovery by the British archeologist Dame Kathleen Kenyon of rock-cut tombs that date from about 1800 to 1650 BC. The dead were buried with most of their earthly possessions, which give vital clues to life in these times. Among the articles found were pottery, carved wooden furniture, weapons, and ornaments such as jewelry boxes carved from bone. Remarkably, a unique combination of soil and weather conditions has preserved organic materials, so that bowls of fruit, cereal, and meat have survived, as well as scraps of textiles and hair.

The city Joshua destroyed

It was in the 13th century BC that the Israelites entered the land of Canaan and Joshua's army defeated and destroyed Jericho. The site has long been identified with a mound known as Tell es-Sultan, where excavations in the 1930s by Professor John Garstang unearthed the remains of a city wall that had apparently collapsed, along with signs of a huge fire. It was assumed that this was evidence of the story of Joshua, but Kathleen Kenyon's excavations in the 1950s proved that the wall was in fact much earlier, from the Early Bronze Age town that was invaded in 2300 BC.

Kenyon's findings have given rise to various theories about the fall of Jericho under Joshua. One possibility is that the story has no real factual basis; another is that the site of Joshua's city was elsewhere; a third and probably the most likely theory is that massive erosion of the top of the mound by rain and wind has destroyed all evidence of the city of Joshua's time. In any case it looks as though the possibility of ever finding evidence of Joshua's Jericho is remote.

When Joshua destroyed Jericho he put a curse on anyone who attempted to rebuild the city: whoever laid the foundations would lose his eldest son, and whoever built the gates would lose his youngest son (Joshua 6:26). Perhaps daunted by this, nobody disturbed the ruins for some 400 years. In about 870 BC, during the reign of King Ahab, Hiel the Bethelite rebuilt the city and lost his eldest and youngest sons in the process, thus fulfilling Joshua's curse (1 Kings 16:34). It was in Hiel's city that the prophets Elijah and Elisha lived, and Elisha "healed" the town's water, making it wholesome (2 Kings 2:4–5, 19–22). Zedekiah, the last king of Judah, was captured in the plains of Jericho by the Babylonians (2 Kings 25:5), and the city was probably destroyed along with Jerusalem in the Babylonian attack of 586–7.

Herod's Jericho

By New Testament times Jericho had been rebuilt about a mile (1.6 km) south of the old city. Herod the Great had established a winter palace there, where he died in 4 BC. It was common for rich people to move from Jerusalem to Jericho for the winter, because while it can snow in a Jerusalem winter, in the desert of Jericho only 17 miles (27 km) away the temperature is a pleasant 65–68°F (18–20°C). The palace was built astride the banks of the Wadi Qilt and fed with water through aqueducts. The site has revealed evidence of a magnificent building in the Roman style, with rows of decorative niches designed to hold statues, an ornamental water garden, two courtyards, and a swimming pool. The Jewish historian Josephus recounts that Herod had his brother-in-law, the high priest Aristobulus, drowned in the pool. The successors of Herod the Great continued to build on the site.

Jericho is mentioned in several Gospel stories. Jesus met a blind beggar called Bartimeus in Jericho and restored his sight to him (Mark 10:46–52). Perhaps on the same visit to Jericho, Jesus encountered Zaccheus, a rich tax collector who clearly abused his position. Zaccheus was anxious to see Jesus but he was too short to see properly through the crowd, so he climbed a tree to get a better view. Jesus looked up and saw him and told him to come down, for he intended to stay at his house. Despite the crowd's disapproval of Jesus for singling out a known sinner for such an honor, Zaccheus received Jesus in his house and showed his repentance by giving half his goods to the poor and compensating fourfold those he had defrauded. In the parable that Jesus told of the good Samaritan, the man who "fell among thieves" was robbed on the road between Jericho and Jerusalem (Luke 10:30).

The Mount of Temptation outside Jericho, traditionally supposed to be the "exceeding high mountain" where Jesus was tempted by Satan (Matthew 4:8–11), although there is little evidence to support the claim.

The third Jericho

Herodian Jericho eventually fell into ruins. The Crusaders rebuilt Jericho on yet another site, about a mile (1.6 km) east of the Old Testament town, and it is on this site that the modern town stands. During the long period of Turkish rule the city became neglected and depopulated, and by the time of the British mandate it had declined into little more than a village. However, like Herod the Great, the British appreciated the area's warm winter climate and made the town a winter resort.

Jericho became part of Jordan in 1949, after which it expanded considerably. Arab

Right: *Herod's palace in Jericho has been extensively excavated. The main hall, shown here, still bears the imprints of the original decorative floor tiles.*
Below: *The palm trees of modern Jericho frame a scene that does not seem far removed from the Jericho of Bible times.*

Hisham's palace was built by the Umayyad Khalif in AD 724 just outside Jericho. Beautiful mosaics, engravings, and statues were discovered when it was excavated in 1935. The stucco statues of female figures which decorated the palace are typical of the classically influenced Islamic art of the Umayyad period.

refugees poured in from Israel, the town was largely rebuilt, and new irrigation works improved the natural oasis. However, the 1967 Arab–Israeli war depleted the population again. Since 1994 Jericho has been under autonomous Palestinian rule. The present town is of little historical interest to visitors apart from the attractions of the neighboring ancient sites.

Jericho and archeology

The first attempt at excavating Jericho was in the 1860s when Sir Charles Warren's venture proved largely unsuccessful, although one of the shafts he dug was actually within feet (a meter or so) of the Neolithic stone tower later discovered by Kathleen Kenyon. In 1907–9 an Austro–German project under Sellin and Watzinger discovered some thick clay bricks that appeared to be part of a fortifying wall, but the lack of efficient dating techniques meant that they were unable to ascertain whether these were part of the wall from Joshua's time.

The British archeologist Professor John Garstang's excavations from 1930 to 1936 revealed some rock-cut tombs and more of the fortifications. Garstang identified four different stages of building, the last one showing evidence of having been violently destroyed and burnt. He concluded that this last was Joshua's wall; there had probably been an earthquake during which the walls fell down, and Joshua's troops had then captured the city.

This theory stood until Kathleen Kenyon's excavations in the 1950s for the British School of Archaeology in Jerusalem. She used the technique of stratigraphy that she had perfected in collaboration with Sir Mortimer Wheeler. This involved peeling off layers from a mound according to their natural strata, and recording all the details of each layer on the spot. Not only did Kenyon make some invaluable discoveries of Neolithic and Middle Bronze Age settlements in Jericho, but her more sophisticated dating techniques disproved Garstang's theories, showing that the remains he had associated with Joshua's invasion of Jericho dated from some 1,000 years earlier.

Herodian Jericho has been excavated in several projects, particularly by American and Israeli archeologists, and the foundations of the winter palace have been revealed, giving a very clear picture of its design. It shows similarities to other Herodian palaces but differs from them in employing Roman techniques of bricklaying.

Herod's palace in Jericho used the Roman technique known as opus reticulatum, which used pyramid-shaped pieces of stone with square bases that were wedged into the concrete walls.

Excavations of Herod's Jericho. Herod was devoted to the Roman style of architecture, which was reflected in his palace and in other buildings in Jericho.

THE RIVER JORDAN

he Jordan, the lowest river in the world, crosses three countries. It rises on the southern slopes of Mount Hermon in Syria, passes through the former Lake Huleh (now drained) in Israel and feeds into the Sea of Galilee, and then flows into the state of Jordan, draining into the Dead Sea. Although it is only about 75 miles (120 km) from the river's source to the Dead Sea, the Jordan is in fact about twice as long because it is so meandering. The river features in many Bible stories, in both the Old and New Testaments.

This picture by the 16th-century Venetian painter Tintoretto shows Jesus being baptized in the River Jordan by John the Baptist.

Joshua crosses the Jordan

After Moses died Joshua took over the task of leading the children of Israel from their wanderings to the Promised Land of Canaan. They traveled from Shittim, on the plains of Moab, and came to the east bank of the Jordan, where they set up camp. They were near the town of Adam, about 18 miles (29 km) north of Jericho, near the mouth of one of the Jordan's tributaries, the River Jabbok. At this point there is a swift current and the river is difficult to cross, especially in the spring when it tends to flood. Joshua gave the people instructions to follow the priests, who would be carrying the Ark of the Covenant. The priests led the way and came to the river, which had overflowed its banks. As soon as the priests' feet touched it, the water rose up into a pile upstream, cutting off the river at Adam and leaving the riverbed dry. The priests and all the people passed over to the other side of the Jordan (Joshua 3). In 1927 the banks of the Jordan at this very point collapsed after earth tremors, damming the river for about 21 hours, so it is possible that the miraculous crossing involved something of this kind.

Elijah and Elisha

Another miraculous crossing of the Jordan is related in 2 Kings 2, which tells how the great prophet Elijah handed on his ministry to the younger prophet Elisha.

Elijah, knowing that God was sending him on a final journey, tried to say goodbye to Elisha, but Elisha insisted on accompanying him. They traveled together to Bethel, and then to Jericho, and finally to the River Jordan.

When they arrived at the banks of the river, Elijah took off his mantle and struck the water with it. The water divided, so that the two prophets passed across the dry riverbed. When they reached the other side, Elisha asked his mentor to leave him a double portion of his spirit, and Elijah said that if Elisha saw him after he had been taken from him, he would know that this had been granted. Then a whirlwind arose and a chariot of fire drawn by fiery horses appeared, and Elisha saw Elijah taken up with it into heaven.

Elisha took Elijah's mantle, which had fallen when he was taken up, and stood by the banks of the Jordan. As Elijah had done, he struck the waters with the mantle, and was again able to cross on dry land.

John the Baptist

John the Baptist was the prophet and preacher who prepared the way for Jesus. His ministry was based in the area around the River Jordan, where he became renowned for his fierce preaching, urging everyone to repent their sins and be baptized by him in the waters of the Jordan. He quoted the prophet Isaiah, "The voice of one crying in the wilderness, Prepare ye the way of the Lord, make his paths straight." Some people began to wonder whether John was the promised Messiah, but he always insisted that he was only preparing them for the real Messiah (Luke 3:1–18). The account in John the Evangelist's Gospel (1:28) says that John the Baptist was baptizing people at Bethabara (or Bethany in some translations). It is not clear where this was but it is thought to be on the right bank of the river, east of Jericho.

Jesus himself eventually came to John to be baptized, but John was reluctant to do so, saying, "I have need to be baptized of thee, and comest thou to me?" But Jesus insisted, and so John baptized him in the River Jordan. When Jesus rose up from the water, the spirit of God descended on him in the form of a dove, and a voice from the heavens said, "This is my beloved son, in whom I am well pleased" (Matthew 3:13–17).

CAESAREA

The port of Caesarea appears in the Bible as the place where St Paul was imprisoned for two years. Now it is celebrated for its imposing Roman and Crusader ruins.

The aqueduct built by Herod the Great, who founded Caesarea. It brought fresh water to the city from springs located in the hills 10 miles (16 km) away.

Caesarea was founded by Herod the Great on the Mediterranean coast about 23 miles (37 km) south of Mount Carmel. Named in honor of the Emperor Augustus Caesar, it was often called Caesarea Maritima to distinguish it from Caesarea Philippi at the foot of Mount Hermon. The old city was destroyed in the 13th century but is now the site of a kibbutz.

Herod's city

Herod built Caesarea on the site of a Phoenician fortress of the 6th century BC known as Strato's Tower. This stronghold was captured by Pompey; he later presented it to Herod, who began to build a city there in 22 BC. It became the administrative capital for the Romans in Judea and the official seat of both the Roman procurators and the Herodian dynasty. Pontius Pilate was in residence there in Jesus' time.

Caesarea, on the route between Egypt and Tyre, was an important trading post as well as a busy port and naval base. There was an artificial harbor with breakwaters built of immense stone blocks, and an aqueduct that brought water from nearby springs. The city fronted the harbor and was magnificently furnished with public buildings, a large amphitheater, and a temple dedicated to Rome and to Augustus Caesar which enclosed huge statues of the emperor.

Caesarea was the principal port of Judea in Roman times. The port was rebuilt by the Crusaders in the 12th century.

*The reconstruction
shows the city built by
Herod the Great, with
its artificial harbor
formed by huge stone
breakwaters.*

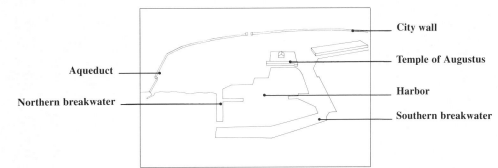

Aqueduct

Northern breakwater

City wall

Temple of Augustus

Harbor

Southern breakwater

The gatehouse dating from the Crusader period in Caesarea. The architecture is typical of the Gothic style favored by the Crusaders.

Philip, Peter, and Paul

Caesarea, with its mixed population of Gentiles and Jews, was one of the centers of the early Christian Church. It is mentioned often in the New Testament Book of Acts, first in connection with the deacon Philip (8:40) who lived in the city with his four daughters – all of whom had the gift of prophecy – and gave hospitality to Paul, Luke, and others (21:8–9).

The Apostle Peter baptized the Roman centurion Cornelius in the city (Acts 10); it was perhaps at Cornelius' house or at Philip's that Peter stayed when he fled to Caesarea after he had been miraculously delivered from prison (12:19). Caesarea is also of significance in the life of Paul, who used the city as a staging post after his second and third missionary journeys (18:22, 21:8). While staying with Philip, Paul met a prophet who predicted that he would be imprisoned if he went to Jerusalem, but he persisted in his resolve to go there. Paul was arrested in Jerusalem and brought before the council, but the Roman authorities arranged for him to be sent to Caesarea for trial before the governor Felix.

Paul was held at Caesarea until the high priest and his supporters arrived from Jerusalem to make their case against him as a rabble-rouser. Felix heard their accusation and

Inset: *Coin minted during the reign of Septimus Severus, Roman emperor AD 193–211.* **Right:** *Inscription found in Caesarea in 1961. It dates from AD 26–36 and refers to Tiberius (emperor at the time) and to "Pontius Pilate, prefect of Judea."*

Paul's defense and he imprisoned Paul. Felix was succeeded as governor by Festus, who now had to deal with this controversial prisoner. When King Agrippa arrived in Caesarea Festus handed the case over to him, and Paul made his defense again before the king, who was moved by his eloquence and would have released him had it not already been agreed that Paul would be sent to Rome for trial (Acts 25, 26).

Rebellion and decline

Caesarea was the center of a Jewish revolt against Rome in AD 66, when many of the Jewish population were massacred. After the Bar Kokhba rebellion of 130–35 ten Jewish leaders were executed. However, Caesarea continued to flourish under the Romans, and then as part of the Byzantine Empire.

The city had declined under Arab rule when it was taken by the Crusaders at the beginning of the 12th century. They rebuilt and fortified the port and citadel, creating a much smaller city whose walls and moat remain today. In 1265 the Mamluks took the

THE CONVERSION OF CORNELIUS

The story of Cornelius, the first Gentile convert, is told in Acts 10. He was a Roman centurion living at Caesarea, who is described as "a devout man." One day Cornelius had a vision in which he saw an angel of God appear and address him by name. The angel told him that God approved of his prayer and charitable works and instructed him to send men to Joppa to fetch Peter, who would tell Cornelius what to do.

Meanwhile, Peter too had a vision. He saw a great sheet being lowered down to earth from heaven, and inside it were all kinds of animals and birds, including some that were unclean according to Jewish dietary law. A voice said, "Rise, Peter, kill and eat." Peter protested that he had never eaten anything that was unclean, but the voice told him that anything that God had cleansed was no longer unclean.

This painting by the Italian artist Bernardo Cavallino shows St Peter with Cornelius and members of his household or entourage, who appear to be variously enthralled by or indifferent to his conversion.

While he was still wondering what the vision signified, Cornelius' messengers arrived, and told him about Cornelius'

vision. The next morning they set off for Caesarea. When Peter arrived he told Cornelius that although it was against Jewish law for him to enter a Gentile's house, God had just revealed to him that he should not consider anyone unclean. Cornelius described his vision and asked Peter what message he had for him from God. Peter then told Cornelius and his family and friends about Jesus' death and resurrection, and how salvation could be found through belief in him.

As they were listening the Holy Spirit came upon Cornelius and his household and they began praising God and speaking in tongues. Peter declared that though these were Gentiles nobody could deny them baptism, as they had already received the Holy Spirit. So Cornelius and all his household were baptized as Christians, and Peter stayed with them for several more days.

city and destroyed most of it, after which it remained a ruin until the 19th century. From 1884 to 1948 it was a Bosnian Muslim settlement. In 1940 the kibbutz of Sedot Yam was founded just south of the original city. The new settlers have built a jetty over the Roman and Crusader breakwaters, and modern hotels and a golf course lie beside the ruins of the old city.

Excavations started on the site in 1948, since when Israeli and Italian archeologists have made many important discoveries including a Roman temple, amphitheater, and hippodrome (racecourse), as well as the original stone jetties of Herod's harbor, and a Latin inscription referring to Pontius Pilate.

TYRE

Once the major seaport of the Phoenician coast, Tyre was the home of the infamous Jezebel and the setting for one of Jesus' miracles.

The city originally had two harbors, one on the mainland and the other on an island just off the shore, but the island has long since become a peninsula. Once a major city-state, Tyre is now no more than a small town in southern Lebanon which has been torn apart in recent years by the conflict in the Middle East.

Tyre and Sidon

Tyre lies about 20 miles (32 km) south of the coastal town of Sidon, and has always been closely associated with it. The Bible often uses the two names synonymously, and the Phoenician people in general were often referred to as "Sidonians." The Phoenicians, Israel's closest neighbors in the north, were a seafaring merchant people. In fact they were Canaanites, inhabiting part of the land originally promised to the Israelites, though never claimed during Old Testament times. While Tyre is an ancient city (the historian Herodotus claims that it was founded about 2700 BC), Sidon is even older and it is probable that Tyre was built as a colony of Sidon. The two cities were for centuries subject to Egyptian rule, having been captured because of their strategic location for trade. Tyre is mentioned in many

The sunken remains of what was once the great Phoenician harbor.

Flowers blooming among the ruins of ancient Tyre.

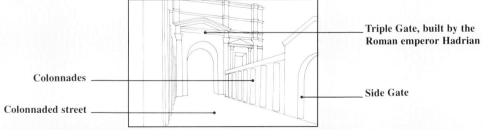

A reconstruction of Hadrian's Gate and a colonnaded street built by the 1st-century AD Roman emperor Hadrian who traveled widely in Palestine and the surrounding countries.

Triple Gate, built by the Roman emperor Hadrian

Colonnades

Colonnaded street

Side Gate

One of the cedars of Lebanon for which Tyre was famous. They were used in the building of Solomon's Temple.

ancient Egyptian inscriptions. In 1200 BC Sidon was sacked by the Philistines. Most of the Sidonians fled to Tyre, which from that time began to surpass its neighbor in importance. From about the 10th century BC it became independent of Egypt, whose influence over Phoenicia had waned, and was protected by strong fortifications: "the stronghold of Tyre" is mentioned in 2 Samuel 24:7.

Tyre and Israel

Tyre features in the Old Testament mainly in connection with the reign of its second independent king, Hiram I, who brought in Tyre's "golden age." He built a causeway linking the mainland and the island harbors. Trade flourished, thanks to Tyre's natural resources of timber – particularly the famous cedars of Lebanon – and the shipping fleet which traded all over the Mediterranean. There are many contemporary representations, some of them Egyptian, of Phoenician trading ships with round bows and double banks of oars. The city was also famous for its glassware and for the purple and scarlet dyes that it produced, which were generally known as "Tyrian" and manufactured from mollusks found off the coast.

Although Hiram built temples to the local god Melqart – the Phoenician Baal – and to the goddess Astarte, he was a good friend of

There are two notable figures in the Old Testament who came from Tyre. Both had close associations with kings of Israel, but otherwise they are sharply contrasted. One, Hiram, was a friend of Israel; the other, Jezebel, was one of its enemies.

Hiram was king of Tyre during the city's "golden age," which coincided with the reigns of David and his son Solomon in Israel. After David had been anointed king of Israel at Hebron, he captured Jerusalem and settled there. King Hiram of Tyre then sent a deputation to David, made up of skilled carpenters and masons. They brought with them some of the cedars for which Tyre was famous, and proceeded to build a house for David (2 Samuel 5:11).

Hiram had a great affection for David, and when he heard that Solomon had been

HIRAM AND

anointed as his successor, he sent ambassadors to see how he could be of service to him. Solomon sent word to Hiram that he intended to build a temple and he would like Hiram to provide wood and skilled artisans to help in its construction. Hiram was very willing to help in this way and it was agreed that he would supply the cedar and fir trees and send workers to Solomon, who in return gave Hiram wheat and oil (1 Kings 5:1–11). This was just one of many mutually beneficial trading treaties that linked Hiram to Solomon. Twenty years after their first arrangement Hiram visited Solomon to see the Temple and to look at the 20 towns in Galilee that Solomon had given him in exchange for a large amount of gold (1 Kings 9:10–14). He was unimpressed by the towns, and did not hesitate to say so, but this did not appear to cause any rift between the two kings, who continued their fruitful relationship. Solomon's ships used to join Hiram's fleets in trading expeditions, returning laden with "gold and silver, ivory, and apes, and peacocks" (1 Kings 10:21–22).

An engraving by the 19th-century French illustrator Gustave Doré shows cedars of Lebanon being cut down for the construction of Solomon's Temple.

The remains of a colonnaded street from the Roman period that began in 68 BC.

JEZEBEL

Jezebel was the daughter of Ethbaal, who was priest-king of Tyre and Sidon some 50 years after Hiram's reign. Omri, king of Israel, married his son Ahab to her to cement an alliance between the two countries. Jezebel was a fervent worshiper of the Tyrian form of the god Baal, and influenced her husband who, when he became king, set up altars to Baal, and worshiped other pagan gods and goddesses (1 Kings 16: 29–33).

The evil reign of Ahab and Jezebel was punished by a great drought, and this culminated in the famous contest between Elijah and the prophets of Baal on Mount Carmel (1 Kings 18). Elijah was victorious and the drought ended (1 Kings 18:40–45). When Jezebel heard this she threatened to kill Elijah, so that he was forced to flee (1 Kings 19:1–3).

Jezebel next appears in the story of Naboth's vineyard (1 Kings 21). Naboth owned a vineyard on land that Ahab coveted, but refused to sell it to the king. Jezebel forged letters in Ahab's name and bribed two men to accuse Naboth falsely of blasphemy, so that he was stoned to death. She then coolly told her husband to go and take Naboth's vineyard. But Ahab met Elijah in the vineyard, who prophesied doom to the king and told him that "the dogs shall eat Jezebel by the wall of Jezreel."

Ahab and his succesor Ahaziah died, and Jehoram came to the throne. During a battle at Jezreel, Jehoram met Jehu, the man appointed by God to fulfil Elijah's

Another engraving by Gustave Doré showing Jezebel being thrown from her window.

prophecy. "Is it peace, Jehu?" Jehoram asked. Jehu replied, "What peace, so long as the whoredoms of thy mother Jezebel and her witchcrafts are so many?" and killed Jehoram. Jezebel's fate was inevitable but she boldly made up her face, arranged her hair, and looked out from her window as Jehu arrived. Jehu called up, "Who is on my side?" and when some eunuchs appeared at the window he commanded, "Throw her down." They obeyed, and Jezebel's body was smashed against the wall and on the ground beneath, so that there was not enough left of her to be buried (2 Kings 9). Her remains were eaten by dogs, fulfilling Elijah's gruesome prophecy.

Israel and his adherance to pagan gods did not prevent him from assisting in the building of Solomon's Temple. Tyre was also renowned for the skill of its artisans, and when Hiram sent timber to David and Solomon he also sent them skilled workers, not only carpenters but also metalworkers, including one man – also named Hiram – who was responsible for working all the bronze columns and capitals in the temple, as well as decorative carts and basins (1 Kings 7:13–45). Although archeological work in Tyre itself has been very limited, the products of Tyrian artisans have been found in profusion outside Phoenicia. Carved ivory from Ahab's palace has been discovered in Samaria, and Tyrian coins have been found all over the Mediterranean and Middle Eastern areas.

Other Old Testament associations with Tyre are less amicable. The Tyrian princess Jezebel brought her pagan religion to Israel and was ultimately responsible for the destruction of a royal dynasty. Isaiah 23 is devoted to prophecies of doom and destruction for Tyre and Sidon. True to the prophet's

Another view of the colonnaded street, from the days when Tyre was a flourishing commercial city under Roman rule.

colonists from Tyre founded the North African city of Carthage; Virgil's *Aeneid* tells of the Tyrian princess Dido who ruled there.

In 722 BC Tyre, along with Samaria, fell to the Assyrian king Sargon II, and was later threatened by Sennacherib, but managed to escape damage by accepting a new king appointed by the Assyrians. The last Assyrian assault on Tyre came from Ashurbanipal in the 7th century BC, who beseiged the city and massacred many of its inhabitants. After Assyrian power declined, the new threat to Tyre came from the Babylonians. From 587 to 574 BC King Nebuchadrezzar beseiged the city, as predicted by the prophets Jeremiah (27:1–11) and Ezekiel (26–28). The book of Ezekiel condemns Tyre's pride, but also provides us with a vivid picture of its prosperity and abundance.

Greek, Roman, and Muslim Tyre

From 538 to 332 BC Tyre was ruled by Persian kings, but it continued to prosper as a port and trading city. In 322 it withstood the great Macedonian conqueror Alexander the Great in a seven-month siege. Eventually Alexander built a massive mole (breakwater) from the mainland to reach the fortified island and so captured the city. About 10,000 Tyrians were killed and three times that number – mainly women and children – were taken as slaves. The mole that Alexander built remained, and has now permanently converted the island into a peninsula.

Tyre next came under the rule of the Egyptian Ptolemies, and then in 200 BC became part of the Seleucid kingdom. In 68 BC it fell under Roman rule. At that time the city's commercial status rested mainly on

predictions, Tyre did suffer from attack and invasion over the centuries but was never utterly defeated. The Tyrians were forced to pay tribute to the Assyrians, but managed to retain their autonomy. In about 815 BC

TYRE

The east apse of a Crusader church. For nearly 100 years Tyre was part of the Crusader Kingdom of Jerusalem.

a port, but its population and importance have diminished greatly. There has been some archeological research, particularly in the now silted-up and unused harbor on the south side of the peninsula, but as most of the ancient Phoenician city lies beneath the present town it cannot be excavated. Tyre has been much involved in the struggles between Lebanon and Israel, and has suffered from several heavy bomb attacks.

its textile trade, founded on its traditional dyes and on the silk cloth and garments that it produced. Jesus traveled to Tyre and Sidon, and it was here that he met a women who, by her persistence, persuaded him to depart from his usual practice of ministering only to Jews, and to heal her daughter (Matthew 15:21–28). Jesus preached to the Tyrians (Mark 3:8; Luke 6:17) and he accorded Tyre and Sidon the rather faint praise of comparing them, as heathen cities, favorably with the Galilean towns that had heard his preaching but refused to repent (Matthew 11:20–22).

By the 2nd century AD a Christian community had grown up in the city; Origen, the influential Christian theologian, was buried here in AD 254. Tyre was under Muslim rule from 634 until 1194, when the conquering Crusaders made it part of their Kingdom of Jerusalem. The city flourished again as part of the Crusader state, but when the Mamluk Muslims captured it in 1291 it began to decline.

After the breakup of the Ottoman Empire following World War I, Lebanon came under French jurisdiction, and even when it became an independent Arab republic in 1920 it remained under French mandate until 1944. Tyre – whose name is Sur in Arabic – remains

A view of the modern town, still a port, but much diminished in its importance.

Joseph in Egypt

The story of Joseph, told in Genesis 37–50, probably took place some time between 1720 and 1500 BC, the time when the Hyksos dynasty ruled in Egypt. The Hyksos were Semitic in origin, but had adapted completely to Egyptian culture. There is evidence that many Semites of various tribes were taken as slaves to Egypt at that time, and some achieved high office.

Sold into slavery

Joseph was the favorite son of his father Jacob. His father's partiality and his own apparent arrogance earned him the enmity of his ten older half-brothers, who plotted to kill him. Finding him alone, they threw him into a well, but soon after a group of merchants passed by on their way to Egypt. The merchants were happy to buy Joseph to sell as a slave there. The brothers covered up their crime by smearing goat's blood on Joseph's coat so that his father would believe he had been killed by wild animals.

Joseph was sold to Potiphar, one of the Pharaoh's officials. He was so efficient that he was promoted rapidly, and soon was running the whole household. All went well until the handsome young Hebrew caught the eye of Potiphar's wife, who set out to seduce him. Joseph constantly rebuffed her. Infuriated, she told her husband that his Hebrew servant had tried to rape her, and Potiphar had Joseph imprisoned.

A 13th-century mosaic from St Mark's, Venice, showing Joseph and his brothers.

Joseph in prison

Joseph's abilities and intelligence again worked in his favor, and he came to be entrusted with much of the prison's administration. When two of Pharaoh's officials, his chief butler and baker, were imprisoned, Joseph was assigned to look after them. Both had dreams which Joseph interpreted for them. He said that in three days time the baker would be executed but the butler pardoned. Joseph asked the butler to put in a good word for him with Pharaoh, but after his release the man forgot about Joseph.

Two years later Pharaoh himself had strange dreams that all his wise men were unable to interpret. At last the butler remembered the young man who had successfully interpreted his dream in prison. Joseph was sent for and was able to tell Pharaoh the meaning of his dreams. They signified that there would be seven years of good harvests, followed by seven years of famine. Joseph advised Pharaoh to store food during the years of plenty to draw on in the years of famine. Pharaoh was so impressed by Joseph that he made him a governor over Egypt, in charge of organizing the storage of grain.

The brothers in Egypt

There were such bountiful harvests in the first seven years that Joseph was able to provide grain during the famine, not only for the Egyptians, but for people from other countries that were also short of food. One such country was Canaan, and when Jacob heard that grain was obtainable in Egypt he sent his ten older sons there to buy some.

When his brothers appeared Joseph knew them immediately, but they failed to recognize him. He did not acknowledge them, but accused them of being spies. He demanded that they prove their story that they were simply brothers from Canaan come to buy food, and that they should bring Benjamin, Jacob's youngest son and Joseph's only full brother, to Egypt. He forced them to leave one of their number, Simeon, as a hostage. Then Joseph loaded their packs with grain and money, and they returned to Canaan.

Jacob was reluctant to let his sons return to Egypt with Benjamin, but when the famine persisted, he had to let them go. Again Joseph pretended not to recognize them, and tricked them by planting a silver cup in Benjamin's pack and then accusing him of the theft, insisting that he must remain in Egypt as a slave. Judah pleaded for his young brother, telling Joseph it would break their father's heart to lose his youngest son. At last Joseph relented and revealed who he was. He forgave his brothers and loaded them with gifts. Eventually Jacob and all his sons settled in Egypt.

JOPPA

The ancient port from where Jonah set sail, and where the
Apostle Peter performed miracles, is now incorporated into
the modern city of Tel Aviv-Yafo.

The waterfront at Jaffa, once the biblical port of Joppa, and now part of the sprawling city of Tel Aviv-Yafo.

The ancient city of Joppa, on the Mediterranean coast 35 miles (56 km) from Jerusalem, features in both the Old and New Testaments. Now no longer a port, it has merged with the modern Israeli city of Tel Aviv to become part of the large municipality of Tel Aviv-Yafo.

The old harbor town

There are references to Joppa in Egyptian writings of the 14th and 15th centuries BC, but archeological evidence suggests that the town was settled as early as the 17th century BC. The first mention of Joppa in the Old Testament comes in the book of Joshua, which deals with the invasion and division of the land of Canaan. In the continuous struggle between the Israelites and the Philistines the town was captured by the Philistines, but the Israelites were still allowed to use it as a port.

During this time Joppa was influenced by the culture of the seafaring Phoenician peoples, whose territory was based at Tyre and Sidon. Solomon negotiated with the king of Tyre about importing cedars of Lebanon by sea to Joppa for building the Temple. After Solomon's Temple was destroyed, Joppa was used again for the same purpose in the rebuilding of the Temple under Ezra (Ezra 3:7). When Hezekiah was king of Judah, Joppa was one of the towns pillaged by the Assyrian ruler Sennacherib in his third campaign (701 BC).

The final mention of Joppa in the Old Testament comes in the much-loved story of

Boats in the harbor of old Jaffa. The port was closed in 1965 and now the only boats that are found in the harbor are craft used for fishing or recreation.

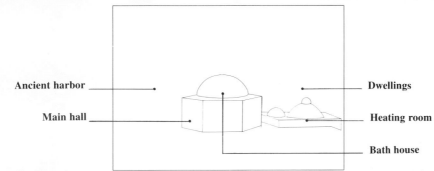

The port of Joppa in New Testament times, showing public baths in the foreground. The view from the old town is now dominated by the skyline of Tel Aviv.

Ancient harbor

Dwellings

Main hall

Heating room

Bath house

THE RAISING OF DORCAS

The first of the New Testament stories about Joppa is told in the book of Acts (9:36–43). When Peter was staying at Lydda, about 11 miles (18 km) inland, a woman called Dorcas died in Joppa. Her Greek name and its Arabic equivalent, Tabitha, both mean "gazelle." Dorcas was a Christian disciple who was renowned for her good works among the poor and her diligence as a needlewoman. When she fell ill and died her grieving friends sent two men to Lydda to summon Peter to Dorcas' house in Joppa. He prayed over her body, then commanded, "Tabitha, arise." She opened her eyes, sat up, and rose to her feet. The miracle was soon known all over the town, so that many people in Joppa came to believe in Jesus.

Peter remained in the town, staying at the house of Simon the tanner. Here he had a vision from God that persuaded him that the old rules of what was clean and unclean no longer applied and, by implication, the Gospel must be open to Gentiles as well as to Jews. This revelation freed him to baptize the Roman centurion Cornelius at Caesarea.

Right: *An illustration from a Victorian Bible showing Dorcas' good deeds among the poor of Joppa.* **Left:** *The house of Simon the tanner, where Peter stayed when he visited Joppa.*

Joppa has seen some interesting archeological discoveries. These excavations are of buildings from Joppa in the 3rd century BC.

Jonah. The prophet was told to go to Nineveh where he should preach repentance to the people, but instead he went down to Joppa and boarded a ship bound for Tarshish.

New Testament times and beyond

In New Testament times Joppa was under Roman rule; it was still inhabited mainly by Jews, but as a major port and trading post it would have had residents and visitors of many nationalities. Joppa is not mentioned in any of the Gospels, but clearly the disciples must have traveled to the town and spread the

word, for a church was already established in the town by the time of the events described in the New Testament book of Acts. All of the stories in Acts that are set in Joppa concern the Apostle Peter. Here he raised Dorcas, and later had the vision that converted him to the belief that the Gospel was also for Gentiles.

In the 2nd century AD Joppa was part of the area in which the Jews revolted against Roman rule; their

Most of the once large Arab population have now left Jaffa, but the great mosque in the old part of the town remains.

Left: *The crowded modern city of Tel Aviv, which has grown from a small suburb to become the largest town in Israel.* **Below:** *A minaret dominates this scene of old Jaffa.*

rebellion was suppressed by the Emperor Hadrian. During the Christian era inaugurated by the Emperor Constantine, the cult of pilgrimages began: now and for centuries to come Joppa became the landing place for pilgrims on their way to Jerusalem and other holy sites. Joppa continued as a port throughout Muslim, Crusader, and Ottoman rule. The town was settled mainly by Arabs, but Jews continued to live there.

The modern city of Tel Aviv-Yafo

When Jews began to settle in Palestine in the late 19th century the ancient town of Joppa (which was now called Jaffa, or Yafa in Arabic) saw Jews and Arabs living peacefully side by side. By the turn of the century, as immigration increased, the Jewish quarter of the town had become seriously overcrowded. The Zionist settlers embarked on the building of a new modern suburb on a barren area of sand dunes northeast of the Jewish quarter.

This suburb, named Tel Aviv, was initially wholly residential. During the British mandate the population of Tel Aviv continued to grow until its dominance provoked riots among the Arabs in Jaffa. The British authorities decided to separate Tel Aviv from Jaffa and give it the status of a town in its own right. With the new flood of European immigrants in the early 1930s, the population of Tel Aviv overtook that of Jaffa. In 1948, when the State of Israel was established, most of the Arab population fled from Jaffa, leaving a largely empty town which quickly filled up with Jewish immigrants. In 1950 Tel Aviv and Jaffa reunited to become Tel Aviv-Yafo.

Tel Aviv-Yafo is now the largest and most important town in Israel. Most of the public and industrial buildings are situated in the

This pottery from the Israelite period was found during excavations at Jaffa.

new part of the city while Jaffa's importance has steadily declined, especially since 1965 when a new port was established at Ashdod and the ancient port of Jaffa was shut down.

Jaffa's main attraction now is for the many tourists who visit the largely unspoiled old town. In Jaffa's old Arab quarter, the houses and workshops appear to have changed little from Biblical times, and Christian pilgrims can visit the house where Simon the tanner lived, and where Peter had his vision.

Jaffa has been the site of various archeological explorations which have revealed evidence of the diverse influences over the centuries. In the first major project in 1873–4 the French archeologist Charles-Simon Clermont-Ganneau, appointed by the Palestine Exploration Fund, found a Jewish necropolis. More recent research has revealed decorated pottery dating from the Philistine settlement at Joppa from about the 12th century BC; a 13th-century temple that appears to be devoted to a lion cult; and evidence of Egyptian influence in the late 13th and early 12th centuries BC in the form of inscribed fragments of stone and metal that once formed part of the city gates.

The Garden of Eden

Perhaps the best-known of all the Bible stories is the very first story from the first three chapters of Genesis, that tells how God created the world and made Adam and Eve. The beautiful garden where Adam and Eve led an idyllic life until their expulsion has been a source of endless fascination for centuries, and has provided inspiration for writers, artists, and theologians.

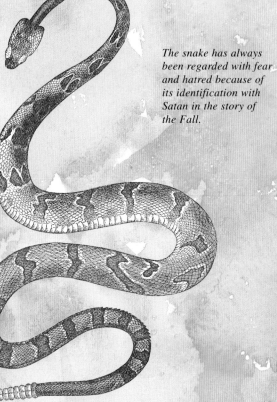

The snake has always been regarded with fear and hatred because of its identification with Satan in the story of the Fall.

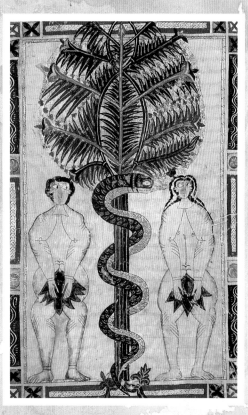

The Creation and Fall

Genesis provides two accounts of the creation of the first man and woman. In Genesis 1 God creates all the animals and plants and then creates both male and female "in his own image," giving them dominion over all the other living things. In Genesis 2 he creates Adam out of dust and places him in the Garden of Eden. He then makes all the other animals, and finally creates Eve from Adam's rib. God had told Adam that he could eat from any tree in the garden except the tree of the knowledge of good and evil, but Eve, tempted by the serpent, ate the fruit of that tree and persuaded Adam to do the same. As soon as they had eaten it they realized that they were naked and made themselves aprons of fig leaves. When God saw this he knew they had eaten the forbidden fruit; he cursed the serpent and drove Adam and Eve from the garden.

This depiction of the story of Adam and Eve comes from a 10th-century Guadalupen manuscript.

Where was the Garden?

Genesis 2:10–14 gives the only clue to the location of the Garden of Eden, naming four rivers that watered it. Only one – the Euphrates – is definitely identifiable, but it is almost certain that Hiddekel is the Tigris. This strongly suggests that the garden was located in southern Mesopotamia, but it is clearly futile to attempt to locate precisely what is clearly a mythical story, albeit an extremely powerful and compelling one. Similar stories exist in other cultures, including a Sumerian myth of an earthly paradise called Dilmun.

The River Tigris, believed to be the Hiddekel of the Bible.

Significance of the Story

The story of the Garden of Eden influenced both Jewish and Christian theology. The garden became identified with paradise in Jewish thought, and Revelation 2:7 mentions the tree of life in paradise. St Paul postulated the idea of Jesus as the "second Adam" (Romans 5:12–21) and uses Eve's disobedience to justify his doctrine on women's submissiveness (1 Timothy 11–14). The serpent reappears in Revelation 12 and 20, metamorphosized into a dragon but still symbolizing Satan, "the deceiver."

16th-century etching of the tree of knowledge. Although the forbidden fruit is traditionally portrayed as an apple, the Bible account does not actually mention apples at all. The only fruit specifically mentioned in the story is the fig, whose leaves were used as the first clothes.

CAPERNAUM

Capernaum, a small town in Galilee, was the base from which Jesus worked throughout his ministry.

The site of Capernaum on the shores of the Sea of Galilee, the town that Jesus adopted as his second home.

Its original Aramaic name has changed little in modern Hebrew – "the town of Nahum." In the Greek of the Gospels it is called Kapharnaoum. The town lies on the northwestern shore of the Sea of Galilee.

Jesus' second home

In Jesus' time Capernaum was the most important of several busy fishing communities clustered along the shores of the Sea of Galilee. It was a trading center and market thronged with merchants and traders from many countries. It was also a garrison town, housing the occupying Roman army and administrative officials. Jesus appears to have lived and preached in Capernaum from the very beginning of his ministry.

Jesus first made his reputation by preaching in the synagogue there; those who heard him were struck by his air of authority (Mark 1:21–2) and by his power to heal (Luke 4:31–9). It was from there that he called his first disciples, the brothers Peter and Andrew and the brothers James and John, all of them local fishermen (Matthew 4:18–22), and later the tax collector Matthew, also called Levi (Matthew 9:9; Mark 2:14). Capernaum was

Most of the recent excavations at Capernaum have been carried out by the members of the Franciscan order. Their church, pictured here, is right on the shores of the Sea of Galilee.

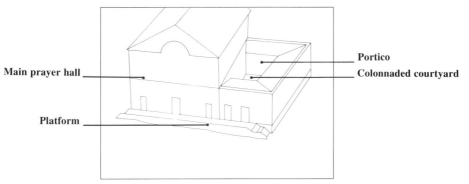

A reconstruction of the synagogue at Capernaum, which was first excavated in 1905. The building probably dates to the 4th or 5th century AD.

Main prayer hall

Portico

Colonnaded courtyard

Platform

127

THE HEALING OF THE PARALYTIC

One of the favorite stories set in Capernaum is told in Mark 2:1–12. Word had got around that Jesus was back in Capernaum, and the house quickly filled with people who were eager to hear him preach. While he was preaching four men approached, carrying a paralyzed man on a stretcher. They found that it was quite impossible to bring the stretcher into the house, for it was tightly packed and the door was blocked, so they removed part of the roof and let down the man on his stretcher through the opening.

When Jesus saw what the man's friends had done, and realized the strength of their faith, he said to the paralytic, "Son, thy sins be forgiven

An engraving of the paralytic man who was lowered down through the roof for Jesus to heal.

thee." Some of the scribes who were in the house were shocked to hear Jesus speak like this, for it was surely blasphemous for an ordinary man to take God's prerogative of forgiving sins. Jesus asked them, "Why reason ye these things in your hearts? Whether it is easier to say . . . thy sins be forgiven thee; or to say, Arise and take up thy bed and walk? But that ye may know that the Son of Man hath power on earth to forgive sins . . ." He turned to the paralyzed man and said to him, "Arise, and take up thy bed and go thy way." The paralytic immediately got up, picked up his stretcher and went out, to the amazement of the assembled crowd.

Columns from the reconstructed synagogue, which had a large colonnaded hall at its center. Only the bases of the columns were standing before the Franciscan reconstruction.

the scene of many healing miracles, including those of the centurion's servant and the official's son, who were both apparently healed from a distance (Luke 7:1–10; John 4:46–53); and it was on the Sea of Galilee near Capernaum that Jesus walked on the water (John 6:16–21). And yet, despite his apparent affection for the place, Jesus once condemned Capernaum because the people there would not repent, despite all that they had seen him do there (Matthew 11:23–4).

After Jesus

Most of what we can learn about Capernaum's history after Jesus' death comes from contemporary written sources, such as the Jewish historian Josephus, whose references

to the town have helped to place it geographically. A later pilgrim, Egeria, visited the town in about 383 and describes a fine synagogue and a church that had been made from a house once inhabited by the Apostle Peter. It is thought that this was the house where Jesus lodged when he lived in the town.

It seems that Capernaum remained almost exclusively Jewish in its population and character. However, there was some Christian influence in the form of Jewish Christian sects, who continued to practice the Jewish Law and did not mix with Gentiles, but believed in Jesus. They are mentioned in the writings of 2nd- and 3rd-century rabbis, and one story from AD 110 describes how a rabbi in Capernaum was incited to break the Sabbath by these "heretics." Even after

Left: The partially restored synagogue discovered in Capernaum. It was first thought to be 2nd or 3rd century AD but is now believed to have been built considerably later.

Constantine became emperor there is no evidence of Capernaum being anything other than a Jewish community until the 5th century. By the time a pilgrim of the late 6th century visited the town, the site of Peter's house had become a basilica.

Findings at the site

For many years scholars disputed the whereabouts of Capernaum. There are enough clues from the Gospel references to the town, and from subsequent writers, to locate it fairly precisely on the northern shores of the Sea of Galilee, and near an important spring, known as Tabgha. Two miles (3.2 km) north of the spring was a mound of ruins known as Tell Hum. Excavations here began in 1905, when German archeologists first discovered the remains of a synagogue, which they dated to the 2nd or 3rd century AD. A Franciscan team continued the excavations from 1968 and have reconstructed the synagogue, and also discovered the remains of houses, indicating continuous occupation for eight centuries.

The reconstructed synagogue reveals a long prayer hall with aisles at the sides, connected to a colonnaded courtyard. Both the hall and courtyard are raised on a high platform, which is reached by a flight of steps. The pilgrim Egeria described the synagogue she visited at Capernaum as being reached by "many steps," which is one of the pieces of evidence that confirms the Tell Hum site as Capernaum. Carvings remain showing various traditional Jewish symbols, such as pomegranates, palm trees, and the Ark of the Covenant. There is also a Gentiles' courtyard with gaming boards carved into the flagstones.

The synagogue at Capernaum is not the one where Jesus preached, but is likely to have been built on the same site. There is now considerable controversy over the dating of the reconstructed synagogue. Since its discovery it has been accepted as being late 2nd or early 3rd century, but the more recent discovery of coins from AD 383–408 embedded in the mortar suggests that the building was actually erected in the late 4th or early 5th century.

Further excavations have revealed the remains of the basilica on the site of Peter's house, as described by the 6th-century pilgrim. It is shaped like a double octagon and has a baptistery and mosaic floor. Between the basilica and the synagogue the remains of several houses, built from the local black basalt, have been unearthed, and millstones and olive presses have been found.

Carvings from the ancient synagogue. The carvings in the lower illustration depict the Ark of the Covenant on wheels.

Carvings in the stonework of the synagogue show palm trees and fruit, and a symbol that might be a form of the Star of David.

THE SAMARITANS

amaria was the capital of the northern kingdom of Israel, and the name was also applied to the surrounding area. The city of Samaria was destroyed by the Assyrians in 721 BC and then rebuilt by Herod. However, the Samaritans who are referred to in the New Testament had their capital in Shechem, which lies to the southeast of Samaria and is now the modern West Bank city of Nablus.

The Samaritans were probably of mixed race, but claimed to be descended from the few Jews who remained in Samaria after the Assyrian conquest. They formed a distinct racial and religious group, worshiping at a temple they had built at Mount Gerizim, near Shechem. By New Testament times there was a great deal of friction between the Samaritans and the Jews of Jerusalem, who did not recognize the Samaritans as Jews and regarded them with contempt. Jesus himself ignored this antagonism, often traveling to Samaritan villages. Luke 17:11–19 tells how Jesus met 10 lepers who begged him to have mercy on them. As they went on their way, they realized that they had been healed; but only one of them turned back to thank Jesus, and that man was a Samaritan.

The good Samaritan

Luke 10:25–37 describes how Jesus was asked by a lawyer what he should do to gain eternal life. Jesus told him that he must love God with all his heart and soul, and love his neighbor as himself. "Who is my neighbor?" the lawyer asked. Jesus answered with a parable.

In Jesus' story, a man was traveling from Jerusalem to Jericho when he fell among thieves. They robbed and stripped him, beat him, and left him half dead on the roadway. A priest walked by but, seeing the wounded man, passed by on the other side of the road. Then a Levite came along, but he too passed by on the other side. Finally a Samaritan man came along, and when he saw the wounded man he had compassion on him. He tended his wounds, put him on his own donkey, and took him to a nearby inn. Before leaving, the Samaritan paid the innkeeper to take care of the wounded man.

Jesus asked the lawyer which of the three men was a neighbor to the man who was mugged, and of course the lawyer replied, "He that showed mercy on him." "Go, and do thou likewise," said Jesus. Apart from the clear moral message of this parable, it is significant that Jesus made the hero of the story a member of the despised Samaritan community.

The Samaritan woman

John 4:4–28, 39–42 relates how Jesus was traveling in Samaria and came to a town called Sychar. Jesus stopped to rest at the well known as Jacob's Well when a Samaritan woman came along, and he asked her to draw him some water. The woman was surprised and asked, "How is it that thou, being a Jew, askest drink of me?" Jesus answered that if she knew who he was she would have asked him for living water; he told her that those who drank the water he gave would never be thirsty again, but would have eternal life.

The woman asked Jesus to give her this water, and he told her to fetch her husband. "I have no husband," she said, but Jesus answered that she had in fact had five husbands and was now living with a man who was not her husband. The Samaritan woman was so impressed by Jesus' powers that she declared he was a prophet. She tried to engage him in theological conversation about the debate between Jews and Samaritans as to where God should be worshiped – at Jerusalem or Mount Gerisim. Jesus told her that this was unimportant, for God was spirit and must be worshiped in spirit and in truth. The woman then mentioned the Messiah, and Jesus said, "I that speak unto thee am he." The woman spread the word about Jesus and many Samaritans came to believe in him as the Messiah. When the disciples found Jesus talking to the woman they were amazed, not just because she was a Samaritan, but because of her sex, for it was unheard of for a Jewish teacher to converse with a woman. The story shows how Jesus disregarded not only the racism of his culture, but its sexism too.

This picture by the Polish painter Henryk Siemiradzki shows Jesus in conversation with the Samaritan woman at the well.

JERUSALEM

Jerusalem is the Holy City for Jews as the site of Solomon's Temple, and for Christians as the scene of Christ's trial, crucifixion, and resurrection.

Inhabited for over 4,000 years, Jerusalem has been under the rule of many different nations and has often been attacked, besieged, destroyed, and rebuilt. It is now a city full of contrast and variety, where modern buildings tower over the old Arab and Jewish quarters that evoke the city's rich Biblical past.

The city of David

The first written reference to Jerusalem is in a text dating back to 2500 BC. There is some evidence of prehistoric settlement, but little is known of the city's early history before the 14th century BC, when Jerusalem was apparently under Egyptian rule. There is no mention of Jerusalem, under that name, in the first five books of the Bible. However, it is believed that Salem, which was ruled by King Melchizedek and is mentioned in Genesis 14:18, is identical with Jerusalem.

At the time when the Israelites entered the land of Canaan, about 1210 BC, Jerusalem was in the hands of a Semitic people called the Jebusites. Their settlement was south of what was to become the Temple platform and ran down to the Pool of Siloam. Although Joshua and his army defeated the Jebusites and their allies in battle, the city

These clay figures of household deities were excavated from the area to the south of Jerusalem that is known to archeologists as the City of David. They date from the "Israelite period" of 10th–8th century BC.

Below: *These coins were issued in Jerusalem during the period of Crusader rule 1099–1187. They bear the insignia of the various Crusader orders.*

Right: *The old city of Jerusalem, with the 7th-century Dome of the Rock in the center.*

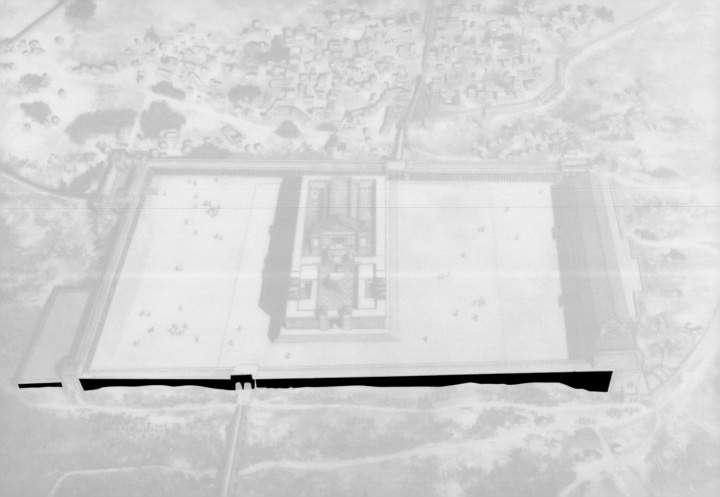

The reconstruction shows the temple built by Herod the Great, on the same plan as Solomon's original temple, though on a grander scale. This is the temple that Jesus attended.

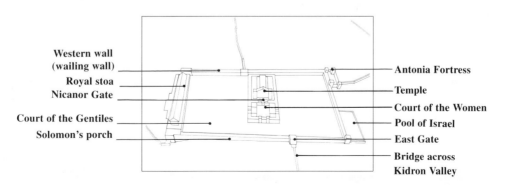

Western wall (wailing wall)

Royal stoa

Nicanor Gate

Court of the Gentiles

Solomon's porch

Antonia Fortress

Temple

Court of the Women

Pool of Israel

East Gate

Bridge across Kidron Valley

The gold-plated wooden chest called the Ark of the Covenant contained the tablets of the law handed down by God to Moses on Mount Sinai. King David took it to Jerusalem and his son Solomon built the Temple to house it.

remained under Jebusite rule (Joshua 15:63), and it was left to David to capture Jerusalem in about 1000 BC (2 Samuel 5).

Under the Jebusites, the city was already known as "Zion" – a word whose meaning is obscure but has remained synonymous with Jerusalem – and now it also acquired the title "City of David." The city became the Israelite capital, where the holy Ark of the Covenant at last found a home. David had the city's fortifications improved and new buildings erected; but it was his son, Solomon, who built the first Temple in Jerusalem. He spared no expense, employing the finest materials and the most expert craftsmen to build and decorate a place fit to house the Ark of the Covenant, which was kept in the inner sanctuary, the "holy of holies" (1 Kings 5–8). Once the Temple was complete the city became a religious center,

where people gathered to celebrate festivals and holy days, and it soon began to acquire symbolic significance as a holy city. The Psalms are full of references to the city, with such memorable exhortations as "Pray for the peace of Jerusalem" (Psalm 122:6) and "If I forget thee, O Jerusalem, let my right hand forget her cunning" (Psalm 137:5).

A city besieged

After Solomon's death around 930 BC the kingdom was divided into two, the northern kingdom of Israel and the southern kingdom of Judah. As the capital of the smaller southern kingdom, Jerusalem declined in importance to some extent. The city was now frequently under attack – by the Egyptians in 922, the Philistines in 850, the northern kingdom in 786, and the Assyrians in 701 – and more than once the palaces and Temple were sacked and looted. In 586 Jerusalem was besieged and captured by the Babylonians,

A wall painting from a 3rd-century synagogue depicting the consecration of the tabernacle and its priests. The tabernacle was a portable sanctuary that was used to house the Ark of the Covenant until Solomon built the Temple.

Below: *This drawing of a pilgrim ship dates from the 4th century AD and was found in the oldest part of the Church of the Holy Sepulcher. The text reads* Domine ivimus, *or "Lord, we went."*

JERUSALEM AND THE CHILDHOOD OF JESUS

A 16th-century portrayal of the Presentation in the Temple, by Dutch painter Jan Provost, showing the infant Jesus held by Simeon.

There are two stories in the New Testament linking the childhood of Jesus to the city of Jerusalem; both are found in the second chapter of the Gospel of Luke.

The first story (Luke 2:22–38) describes how Mary and Joseph had come to the temple in Jerusalem with their baby son in accordance with Jewish law. Mary was attending the temple for a ceremony of purification 40 days after the birth of a child, and offering a sacrifice of two doves (Leviticus 12). She had also come to present her firstborn child Jesus to the Lord, in obedience to the instruction given by God to Moses: "Sanctify unto me all the firstborn" (Exodus 13:2).

In the temple they encountered two elderly people. The first was a very devout old man named Simeon. He was one of those who were daily awaiting the Messiah, "the consolation of Israel," and the Holy Spirit had revealed to him that he would not die before he had seen the Messiah. On the day Jesus was taken to Jerusalem Simeon was guided by the Spirit to visit the temple. When he saw the infant Jesus, Simeon knew that this was the promised one of God, and he took the child in his arms and offered up the prayer that is now known as the Nunc Dimittis.

Also in the temple was an 84-year-old widow called Anna, who was known as a prophetess. She too praised God for the coming of the Messiah, and then spread the word to others with the same hope for the redemption of Israel.

This episode in the life of Jesus is celebrated on February 2 variously as Candlemas, the Purification of the Blessed Virgin Mary, and the Presentation of the Child Jesus. In the Greek Church it is known as *Hypatante*, "meeting," referring to the meeting with Simeon.

In the second story (Luke 2:41–51) Jesus was 12 years old and accompanying his parents to Jerusalem, where they went every year to celebrate the Passover festival. At the end of the feast Mary and Joseph, together with the crowds of other people who had traveled to Jerusalem, were returning home. They assumed that Jesus was somewhere in the crowd, among their family and friends, but after they had been traveling for a day they realized that he was missing.

They retraced their steps to Jerusalem to look for the boy. Only after searching for three days did they find him. He was in the temple, listening to the teaching of the rabbis there, asking them questions and discussing spiritual matters with them. All who heard him were amazed at the maturity of his discourse, but naturally enough Mary's reaction was to rebuke her son for causing so much anxiety. Jesus answered her, "How is it ye sought me? Wist ye not that I must be about my Father's business?" Mary and Joseph could not understand him; but after they returned to Nazareth, Mary "kept all these sayings in her heart."

Jesus Sitting in the Midst of the Doctors by J.J. Tissot, a 19th-century French painter who traveled to Palestine in 1886 and produced a series of watercolors depicting scenes from the life of Christ.

The Garden Tomb, once believed to be the place of Jesus' burial, although the alternative site of the Church of the Holy Sepulcher now seems much more likely.

under their king Nebuchadrezzar; the entire city and the Temple were destroyed, and the people were taken into captivity in Babylon (2 Kings 25).

In 538 Cyrus II of Persia overcame Babylon and allowed the exiles to return to Jerusalem. The Temple was rebuilt (Ezra 1–5) and later, under Nehemiah, the city walls were restored (Nehemiah 3–6). Two centuries later the city came under the rule of Alexander the Great, and subsequently Ptolemy, and then in 198 BC it fell to the Syrians. Again the Temple was desecrated, but after a Jewish revolt under Judas Maccabeus it was rededicated in 165.

Roman rule and the early Church

Jerusalem remained under Jewish rule until it was taken by Pompey in 63 BC. However, Roman influence was countered by the power of the Herodian dynasty; Herod the Great repaired the ravages of the various plundering armies and began the work of rebuilding the Temple on a grand scale, among many ambitious building projects.

Under Herod Jerusalem became great again, but his successors were less competent and Jerusalem became part of a minor Roman

province under the rule of a procurator. So it was when Jesus was exercising his ministry, and it was the procurator Pontius Pilate who sentenced him to death (Matthew 27). The city was the scene of Jesus' trial, crucifixion, and resurrection. Jerusalem became the first center for the early Church (Acts 1–7) until Christians there began to be persecuted; most of them then scattered into other regions to spread the gospel (Acts 8:1). The city was now a symbol of God's glory for Christians as well as Jews, and in the last book of the Bible, John describes his vision of Heaven as "the holy city, new Jerusalem" (Revelation 21:2).

In AD 66 the Jews rebelled against their Roman rulers, and four years later Roman forces under Titus besieged and destroyed the city. There was never to be another Temple in Jerusalem, but the Emperor Hadrian built a new city, Aelia Capitolina, on the site in 130. The layout of this city, on a typical Roman grid plan but smaller than before, is the basis for the modern city center.

After Constantine became emperor in 324 and made Christianity legal, churches and shrines were built and Jerusalem began its "golden age" as a Christian city.

Three faiths

In 638 Jerusalem came under Muslim rule. The great mosque, the Dome of the Rock, was built on the Temple Mount in 691. For some

Above and right: *The Dome of the Rock is built on the rock where Abraham is believed to have prepared to sacrifice Isaac and from where the prophet Muhammad is thought to have ascended to heaven.*

An interior view of the Dome, which is about 60 feet (18 m) in diameter. It is made of wood but is covered in gold leaf and surrounded by a circle of piers and columns.

Jews at the Western Wall, also known as the Wailing Wall. Part of Herod's temple, this is a sacred place for Jews to pray and to lament the destruction of Solomon's Temple.

The Christian quarter in the north-west part of the Old City which contains the Church of the Holy Sepulcher.

Right: *Part of the Muslim quarter in the north-east of the Old City. The different quarters are not sharply distinct: they all have an oriental character and there are mosques outside the Muslim quarter and churches and convents located within it.*

centuries the Muslim rulers were tolerant of the Jews and Christians who lived and worshiped in the city, as well as the many pilgrims who visited it from all parts of Europe. However, in 1071 the Muslims destroyed the Christian shrines and cut off the pilgrim routes. The European powers, with whom the Muslim rule of the Holy City had long been a sore point, decided to invade. In 1099 the Christian army of the First Crusade captured Jerusalem and established a state there; new churches were built and mosques were converted into churches. But in 1187 forces led by Saladin, the Egyptian ruler, regained Jerusalem, which was reestablished as a Muslim city.

Egyptian rule ended in 1517 when Jerusalem was taken by the Turks. For 400 years after that the city was part of the Ottoman Empire, slowly declining in importance. It was primarily a Muslim city, but Jews and Christians lived there and practiced their religion; Christian pilgrimages continued and Jewish immigration increased, particularly during the 19th century. In 1917, following the defeat of the Turks in World War I, Jerusalem came under British mandate.

Jerusalem in the 20th century

British rule in Jerusalem lasted until 1948, by which time the Zionists and Arabs were fighting each other, and both were fighting the British. Eventually the city was split between Israel and Jordan. After the Six Day War in 1967 Israeli troops won control of the whole city, but it remains an area of disputed claims. Although the Israelites regard it as their capital city it is not internationally recognized as such, and many international organizations and foreign embassies are sited in Tel Aviv rather than Jerusalem. The Israelis have expanded the city and erected many modern buildings, including government offices, cultural institutions, and extensive housing projects.

The Old City has been preserved intact. Although it is now only a small district of Jerusalem, it is by far the most interesting part of the city for both tourists and pilgrims. Divided roughly into Jewish, Muslim, Christian, and Armenian quarters, the Old City is essentially Oriental in character with narrow streets and bustling bazaars and markets. Dominated by the Dome of the Rock and the adjacent al-Aqsa mosque, it is also crowded with churches and ancient synagogues and Jewish study houses. The focus of Jewish pilgrimage is the Western Wall (or Wailing Wall), all that remains of Herod's Temple, where Jews pray and lament the destruction of Solomon's Temple.

Christian holy places include the Church of the Holy Sepulcher, believed to be the site of Christ's crucifixion and burial – especially since modern research has established that the church is situated outside the perimeters of the original city walls.

The fact that Jerusalem has been continuously inhabited since the 2nd century AD makes archeological work difficult. Excavations began there in the 19th century and have continued to the present day, particularly since the Six Day War, with most of the work concentrated on the Temple Mount area. Extensive research into ancient documents has helped to reveal many clues to the structure and history of the Holy City over the vicissitudes of 4,000 years.

The Passion of Jesus

The Passion is the term applied to the sufferings of Jesus from his prayers in the Garden of Gethsemane, to his arrest, trial, journey to Calvary, and finally his crucifixion. It is sometimes extended to include the Last Supper. All these events took place in Jerusalem, but there has been much dispute as to the exact site of some of them.

The Crucifixion *by Bartolomé Esteban Murillo, 17th century.*

The Garden of Gethsemane

After the last Passover supper, Jesus took Peter, James, and John and went out to the Mount of Olives, and then to the nearby Garden of Gethsemane. Here Jesus, knowing the sufferings he was to undergo, prayed in anguish while his exhausted disciples slept. Finally he woke them but, as they left the garden, Judas appeared with the chief priests. He greeted Jesus with a kiss, by which sign the priests knew which was the man they had come to arrest (Mark 14:26–50). The Mount of Olives was originally beyond the city, beyond the Kidron valley. The traditionally accepted site for the Garden of Gethsemane is an olive grove on its western slopes.

The Trial

Jesus was taken for trial by the Roman Governor Pontius Pilate. Pilate questioned Jesus and, although it was clear that he was innocent, reluctantly condemned him to death to appease the priests and the rabble (Mark 15:1–15). The traditional site for the trial is the fortress by the Temple Mount, near which is the Ecce Homo ("Behold the man") arch, where Pilate is believed to have shown Jesus to the crowd (John 19:5). Many scholars, however, now think that Pilate would have tried Jesus at his headquarters in Herod's palace, which was on the northwest side of Jerusalem.

The Crucifixion

Jesus was whipped and mocked by the Roman soldiers, who made him a crown of thorns. He was then taken to the place of crucifixion – Calvary or Golgotha – where he was nailed to the cross and left to die in agony, along with two criminals who were being similarly punished (Matthew 27:50). The traditional route to Calvary is the Via Dolorosa but, if the scholars who believe that Jesus was tried in Herod's palace are right, this is not the actual route Jesus would have taken. There is general agreement that the site of Calvary and Jesus' burial place was where the Church of the Holy Sepulcher now stands.

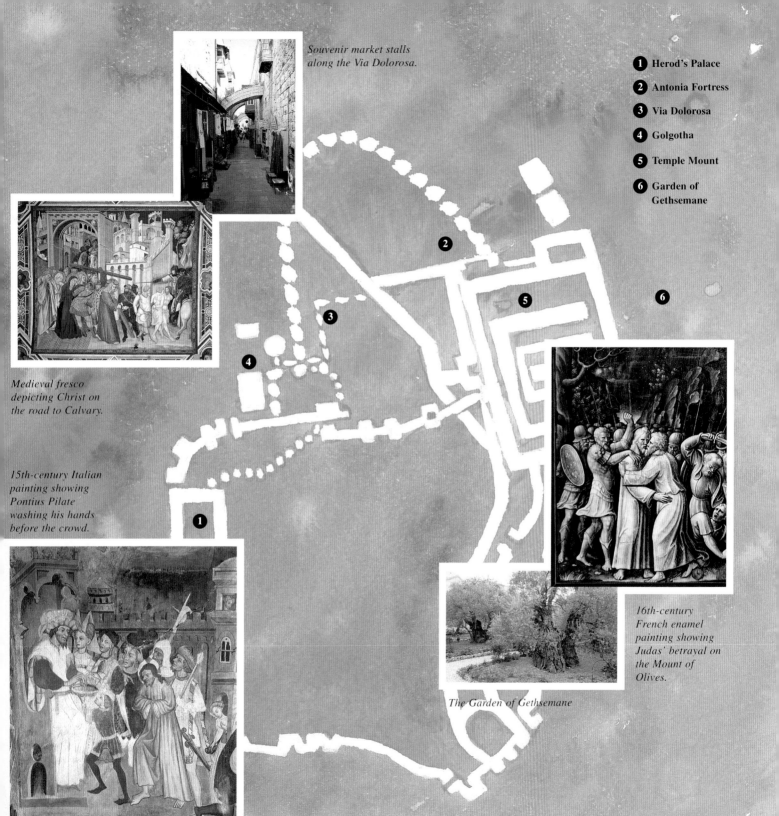

Souvenir market stalls along the Via Dolorosa.

1 Herod's Palace
2 Antonia Fortress
3 Via Dolorosa
4 Golgotha
5 Temple Mount
6 Garden of Gethsemane

Medieval fresco depicting Christ on the road to Calvary.

15th-century Italian painting showing Pontius Pilate washing his hands before the crowd.

16th-century French enamel painting showing Judas' betrayal on the Mount of Olives.

The Garden of Gethsemane

INDEX

Page numbers in *italics* refer to captions and illustrations

A

Aaron 62
Abraham 9, 14, 36, 40, 54, 89
Absalom 41, *41*
Achan 94
Acropolis 28, *28*, 32, 35, *35*
Adam 122–3
Aelia Capitolina 138
Aeschylus 32
agriculture 12
Agrippa, King 104
Ahab, King 59, 60, 88
Ahasuerus, King 78–9
al-Hillal 18
al-Khalil 40
Alexander the Great 24, 60, 84, 112, 138
Amorites 95
Anak, people of 40
Ananias 60
Antioch 60, 85
Aphrodite *13*, 80, 85, *86*
Apollo *80, 86*
Apostles 9, 10, 12
Aram 54
Aramaic language 59
Arameans 54, 59
Ararat, Mount 52
archeology 13–15
architecture 11
Aretas, King 60
Aristophanes 32
Aristotle 32
Ark of the Covenant *52–3*, 53, *129*, 136, *136*
Artemis (Diana) 64, *64*, 68, 69
Artemis, Temple of 64, 69
Ashdod 42
Ashkelon 42
Ashurbanipal 76, 112
Ashurnasirpal II 70
Asia Minor 12
Assyria 9, 13, 70, 74
Assyrians 12, 22, 23, 59, *76*, 77, 84, 112, 130, 136
Astarte 54, 110
Athene 28, *28*
Athens 28–35, *28, 29–31, 32*
Augustus Caesar 50, 100

B

Baal 54, 88
Babylon 9, 13, 14, 15, *17–19*, 18–25, *22, 24, 25*

Hanging Gardens 24, 25
Babylonians 12, 53, 76, 112, 136–8
Bar Kokhba 50, 104
Bar-Jesus 85
Barnabas 80, *84*, 85–6
baths *48*
Bedouin tents *8*
Belshazzar 23, 24
Ben-Hadad, King 59
Bethlehem 44–51, *44, 45–7, 50, 51*
Bible, times of 9–10
Boaz 44
British 36, 40, 50, 86, 96, 121, 139
Bronze Age 11, 80, 87, 95
Byzantium 60, 86, 104

C

Caesarea 100–5, *100, 101–3, 104*
Calah 77
Caleb 40
Calvary 140
Canaan 8, 11, 42, 116
Canaanites 95
Capernaum 26, 124–9, *124, 125–7, 128, 129*
Carmel, Mount 88
Chaldeans 60
Christianity 33, 68, 69, 85
cities 12–13
Clermont-Ganneau, Charles-Simon 121
cloth manufacture 12
Code of Laws 22
Constantine I 50, 121, 138
copper 80, 84
Corinth, Temple of Apollo *10*
Cornelius 104, 105, 120
cosmetic artifacts *11*
Creation 122–3
Crimean War 50
Croesus 64
Crucifixion 138, 140
Crusaders 40, 86, 96, *100*, 113, *132*, 139
cuneiform writing 24
Cyprus 80–7, *80, 81–3, 84, 85, 86*
incense burner *11*
Cyrus II (the Great) *22*, 24, 64, 138

D

daily life 11–12
Damascus 54–61, *54, 55–7, 59, 60, 61*
Daniel 22–3, *22*
Darius the Mede 23, 24
David, King 36, 40, 41, 43, *43*, 44, 48, 59,

110, 111, 136
Dead Sea Scrolls 14–15
deities, household *132*
Delilah 43
Diana *see* Artemis
Dido 112
disciples 124
Dorcas 120, *120*

E

Eden, Garden of 122–3
Edomites 40
Egeria 128, 129
Egypt 9, 11, 13, 14, 60, 62–3, 114–15
Exodus from 9, 63
Egyptians 84, 136
Ekron 42
Elamites 22, *76*
Elgin marbles 34
Elijah 59, 88, 95, 98–9
Elisha 58, *58*, 59, 95, 98–9
Elishah 84
En-Gedi 53
Enosis 86–7
Ephesus 15, 64–9, *65–7, 69*
Epic of Gilgamesh 22, 77
Epicureans 33
Epicurus 32
Esarhaddon 23, 76
Esther 78–9, *79*
Euphrates, River 18, 24, 25
Euripides 32
Eve 122–3
Ezekiel 112

F

family life 11
feeding the five thousand 27
fishing 12
footwear *12*
French 60, 113

G

Galilee, Sea of 12, 26–7
Garden of Eden 122–3
Garden of Gethsemane 140
Garstang, Professor John 97
Gath 42
Gaza 42, 43
Gehazi 58
Gethsemane, Garden of 140
Gibeon 40

Gibeonites 36
gold artifacts, from tombs *34*
Golgotha 140
Goliath 43, *43*
Goths 69
Greece 12–13
Greeks 61, 86
Guy de Lusignan 86

H

Hadad 54
Hadadezer, King 59
Hadrian, Emperor *14*, 33, 50, 86, 123, 138
Haman 79
Hammurapi (Hammurabi) 18, 22, 70
Hanging Gardens of Babylon 24, 25
Hazael 59
Hebrew language 59
Hebron 36–41, *36, 37–9, 40, 41*
Helena (mother of Constantine) 50
Hellenistic period 32
Herod the Great 10, 14, 40, 48–50, 96, *97*, 100, *100*, 130, 138
Herodium *48*, 50
Herodotus 25, 32, 106
Heruli 33
Hezekiah, King 23, 40, 74
Hiram I 110, 111
Hittites 22
Hoham, King 40
Holy Land 8
housing 11, 61, 87
Hyksos dynasty 114

I

incense burner *11*
Isaac 36, *36*
Isaiah 23, 59, 74
Ishtar, statue *23*
Ishtar Gate 24, *24*, 25
Islam (Muslims) 40, 60, 86, 113, 138–9
Israel, kingdom of 8, 10, 40, 59, 136
Israel (modern) 9, 139
Israelites 40, 53, 94, 116
ivory 111

J

Jacob 36, 114, 115
Jebusites 132, 136
Jehu 77, *77*
Jeremiah 112
Jericho 11, 14, 90–97, *91–3, 95, 96, 97*

Jerusalem 8, 10, 11, 40, 48, 132–9, *132, 133–5, 138, 139*
Jesus 9, 10, *15*, 26–7, 96, 99, 113, 124, 128, 130–1, *131*, 137, 138
 birth 44, 48–50, 51
 miracles 27, 96, 128
 Passion 138, 140
Jews 8–9, 41–2, 68, 86, 104, 138
Jezebel 88, 106, 111
John the Baptist 61, *61*, 99
Jonah 70, 75, *75*, 116, 120
Joppa 116–21, *116, 117–19, 120, 121*
Jordan 9, 50
Jordan, River *12*, 26, 98–9, *98*
Joseph 9, 11, 114–15, *114*, 137
Josephus 13, 96, 128
Joshua 36, 40, 85, 90, 94, 97, 98, 132
Judah, kingdom of 8, 10, 40, 48, 59, 136
Judas Maccabeus 40, 138
Justinian, Emperor 50, 51

K
Kassites 22
Kenyon, Dame Kathleen 14, 95, 97
Kition 84, 87
Kittim (Chittim) 84
Kouklia 85, 87, *87*

L
Lachish 77
Layard, Sir Austen Henry 77
Leah 36
Lebanon 9
lions, in sculpture *23, 24*
Lot 54
Lysimachus 64

M
Magi 49
Makarios, Archbishop 87
Mamre 36, 41
Marathon, Battle of 28
marriage 11
Mary, Virgin 48–9, 51, 137
Masada 14
 artifacts from *11, 12*
Medes 76
Melchizedek, King 132
Melqart 110
Mesolithic 90
Mesopotamia 14
Micah 48, 49
mining 12
miracles 27, 96, 120, 128
Mnesicles 28
Mordecai 78–9, *79*
Moriah, Mount 89

Moses 8, 9, 36, 62–3, 88, 98
mosques *22, 41, 61, 120*
mountains, of Old Testament 88–9
Muslims *see* Islam
Myceneans 80

N
Nabateans 60
Nabopolassar 23
Nahum 76
Namaan 58
Naomi 44
Nebuchadrezzar I 22
Nebuchadrezzar II (Nebuchadnezzar) 23–4, 25, 48, 112, 138
Neolithic 80, 90
New Testament 9, 10
Nimrod 18, 70
Nimrud 77
Nineveh 13, 14, 15, 70–7, *71–3, 74, 76*, 120
Noah's Ark 52

O
occupations 12
Old Testament 8–9, 10
 lost treasures 52–3
 mountains of 88–9
Origen 113

P
Palestine 8, 12, 42
Paphos 9, 85, 87, *87*
Parthenon 28, *28*, 32, 34, *34*, 35
Passion 140
Passover 63
Patriarchs 8, 9
Paul *9*, 12, 28, 32–3, *33*, 60, 61, 64, 68, *68*, 69, 85–6, 104
Peloponnesian War 32
Pergamum 64
Pericles 32
Persia 9
Persian Empire 78–9
Persians 24, 28, 60, 64, 84, 112
Peter 104, 105, 116, 120, 121, 124
Petrie, Sir William Flinders 13
Philip 104
Philistines 42–3, 44, 116, 136
Phoenicians 84, 87, 106, 116
Pilate, Pontius 100, *104*, 105, 138, 140
pilgrimages 121, 139
plagues 62–3
Plato 32
Pompey 100, 138
Potiphar 114–15
pottery 87, 95, *121*
 dating 13

prehistory 9
Ptolemies 32, 84, 112, 138
Purim 79
pyramids 11

Q
Qumran 14

R
Rachel 44, *44*
Rameses II 62
Rebekah (Rebecca) 36, *36*
Red Sea 63
Reheboam 48
religion 13, 33
Rezon 59
Richard I of England 86
Rimmon 54
Roman Empire 9, 12–13, 138
Romans 12, 14, 32, 40, 60, 64, 69, 84–5, 86, 87, 100, 104, 112
Ruth 44

S
Saladin 61, *61*, 139
Salamis *84*, 85, 86, *86*, 87
Salem 132
Samaria 10, *61*, 130
Samaritans 130–1
Samson 42–3
Samuel 44
sandals *12*
Sarah (wife of Abraham) 36, 40, *40*
Sargon I *70*
Sargon II 70, 84, 112
Saul, King 43
Saul of Tarsus *see* Paul
Scheil, Jean Vincent 22
Scythians 76
Sea of Galilee 12, 26–7
Sedot Yam 105
Seleucia 24
Seleucids 60, 112
Sennacherib, King 23, 74–6, *74*, 77, 112, 116
Sergius Paulus 85
"Seven Sleepers" 69
Shechem 11
Sidon 106, 116
Sinai, Mount 88, *88*
Sinai region *8*
Sinsharishkin 76
Solomon 11, 53, 59, 110, 111, 116, 136
 Temple 11, 53, 110, 111, 116, 136, 138, 139, *139*
Sophocles 32
Spartans 32

Stoics 33
stratigraphy 14, 97
Strato's Tower 100
Sumuabum, King 18
synagogues *128*, 129, *129*
Syria 9, 54, 60

T
Tanis 6
taxes 12
Tel Aviv-Yafo 116, *116*, 121
Tell es-Sultan *90*, 95
Tell Shalem, statue found at *14*
Temptation, Mount of *96*
Ten Commandments 88
theaters 35, *35*
Tiberias 26
Tiglath Pileser I 70
Tiglath-Pileser III 59
tombs 95
Tombs of the Patriarchs *36*, 40, *40*
Torah *9*
Tower of Babel 18, *18*, 24, 25
towns 11
trade 12
travel 12
Turks 34, 35, 60, 86
Tutankhamun 14
Tyre 106–13, *106, 107–9, 111, 112, 113*, 116

U
Umayyad period 97
Ur of the Chaldees 14

V
Venetians 34, 86

W
Walking on water 27, 128
Warren, Sir Charles 97
West Bank 41, 50
Wheeler, Sir Mortimer 14, 97
Woolley, Sir Leonard 14

X
Xerxes I 24

Z
Zaccheus 96
Zedekiah, King 95
Zeno 32
Zephaniah 76
ziggurats 18, *18*, 22, 24, 25
Zion 136
Zoan 6

CREDITS

Key: *a* above; *b* below; *c* center; *l* left; *r* right

Jon Arnold 8*cl*; J Catling Allen 8*b*, 9*b*; J Allan Cash 9*ar*; Zev Radovan 10, 11*br*; C M Dixon 11*cr*; Jon Arnold 12*a*; Zev Radovan 12*b*; PictureBank 13; J Catling Allen 14; PictureBank 15; Sipa/Rex Features 18*a*; Chris North/Travel Ink 18*b*; Comstock 21; Ann Ronan at Image Select 22*al*; J Catling Allen 22*cl*; Chris North/Travel Ink 23*a*; C M Dixon 23*b*, 24*al* & *cr*; J Catling Allen 24*br* & *cl*; Sipa/Rex Features 25*bl*; Chris North/Travel Ink 25*r*; Visual Arts Library 26; ET Archive 28*al*; Charles Mahaux/Image Bank 28*ar*; Bill Bachmann/Ace 28*b*; Pictor 31; John Macrae-Brown 32*al* & *cl*; Mansell Collection 32*br*; Bridgeman Art Library 33*br*; Ann Ronan at Image Select 34*ar*; J Catling Allen 34*al* & *cl*; Bernard van Berg/Image Bank 34*br*; Ann Ronan at Image Select 35*al*; Michael Freeman 35*ar*; Zev Radovan 36*l*; Topham Picturepoint 36*r*; Zev Radovan 39, 40*a* & *b*; Mansell Collection 41*a*; Topham Picturepoint 41*b*; Visual Arts Library 43; J Allan Cash 44*al*; Image Select 44*ar*; Zev Radovan 44*br*, 47; J Allan Cash 48*ar*, *bl* & *cl*; Visual Arts Library 49*al* & *br*; J Catling Allen 50*al*; Zev Radovan 50*br*; J Allan Cash 50*cr*; Mansell Collection 51*al*; Jon Arnold 51*ar*; Image Select 51*cr*; ET Archive 52*bl*; Mansell Collection 52–3*c*; Zev Radovan 53*br*; Mauritius/Ace 54*bl*; J Catling Allen 54*ar*, 57, 59*al* & *ar*; J Allan Cash 59*br*; J Catling Allen 60, 61*al*, *bl* & *br*; Visual Arts Library 63; Spectrum 64*al*; Jon Arnold 64*bl*; Pictor 64*br*; J Allan Cash 67; Ann Ronan at Image Select 68*l*; J Allan Cash 68*r*; J Catling Allen 69*al*; Pictor 69*ar*; Jon Arnold 69*bl*; C M Dixon 69*br*; Topham Picturepoint 70, 73; Mansell Collection 74*ar*; Spectrum Colour Library 74*b*; Ann Ronan at Image Select 75; J Catling Allen 76*b*; C M Dixon 76*a*, 77*a* & *b*; Visual Arts Library 79; PictureBank 80*l*; C M Dixon 80*r*; J Catling Allen 83; C M Dixon 84*al*; J Catling Allen 84*br* & *cl*; J Allan Cash 84*cr*; Mansell Collection 85; PictureBank 86*al*; Pictor 86*br*; J Allan Cash 86*cl*; PictureBank 87*a*; J Allan Cash 87*b* & *c*; ET Archive 88; Jon Arnold 89*br*; Visual Arts Library 89*l*; Zev Radovan 90*a*, *c* & *l*, 93; Ann Ronan at Image Select 94; Zev Radovan 95*al*; Mansell Collection 95*ar*; J Catling Allen 96*bl*; Zev Radovan 96*cl*; Robert Harding Picture Library 96*cr*, 97*br*; J Allan Cash 97*al*; Zev Radovan 97*ar* & *cl*; Visual Arts Library 98; J Catling Allen 100*al*; Zev Radovan 100*b*, 103, 104*al* & *bc*; J Catling Allen 104*br* & 105*br*; Mansell Collection 105; Peter Sanders 106*a* & *b*, 109; Geoff Johnson/Ace 110*a*; Mansell Collection 110*b*; Zev Radovan 111*ar*; Visual Arts Library 111*ac*; Zev Radovan 112; Peter Sanders 113*al* & *br*; Visual Arts Library 115; Jon Arnold 116*al*; J Allan Cash 116*b*, 120*br*; J Catling Allen 120*c*; Zev Radovan 120*cl*; J Catling Allen 120*c*; Andrea Pistolesi/Image Bank 121*ac*; Robert Harding Picture Library 121*al*; Zev Radovan 121*br*; ET Archive 122*bl*; Mansell Collection 122*ar*, 123*b*; Spectrum 123*cl*; Mansell Collection 124*al*; PictureBank 124*b*; Zev Radovan 127; Mansell Collection 128*a*; Zev Radovan 128*b*, 129*ar* & *cr*; J Allan Cash 129*al*; C M Dixon 129*br*; Visual Arts Library 131; Zev Radovan 132*ar* & *bl*; Jon Arnold 132*br*; Zev Radovan 135; Mansell Collection 136*al*; Zev Radovan 136*bl* & *br*; Visual Arts Library 137*al*; Mansell Collection 137*br*; J Catling Allen 138*al*; J Allan Cash 138*bl*; Michael Freeman 138*cl*; Ronald Sheridan/Ace 138*br*; Billie Love Historical Collection 139*al*; Andrea Pistolesi/Image Bank 139*ar*; Michael Freeman 139*cr*; Visual Arts Library 140, 141*cr*; Roger Howard/Ace 141*ac*; ET Archive 141*bl* & *cl*; Zev Radovan 141*br*; Visual Arts Library 141*cr*.

All other photographs are the copyright of Quarto Publishing plc.

Every effort has been made to acknowledge copyright holders. Quarto would like to apologise if any omissions have been made. We would also like to extend our grateful thanks to the Palestine Exploration Fund, London, and Dr Leen Ritmeyer for help and advice kindly given during the preparation of this book.